BELCOLADE

BELGIAN CHOCOLATE & BEER

52 amazing combinations

Michel Eyckerman

Photography Karl Bruninx

Lannoo

Dear Chefs,

It all started about 15 years ago. As a technical advisor in chocolate and patisserie, I often received questions involving varying challenges and opportunities. One day, I received a request from a Belgian gastronomic association to do a tasting session combining chocolate and beer. Many people who know me are aware that I have difficulties saying no, so I took on the challenge. They introduced me to the owner of the innovative brewery ProefBrouwerij in Lochristi, Belgium, and together we embarked on our first experience of combining the beers he brewed with Belcolade Origins chocolate.

We quickly discovered that this was going to be a long journey, with many trials and some errors. I was so impressed by all the flavors that beer reveals, and I learned that the way we taste chocolate and beer has some similarities. Additionally, the processes of brewing and chocolate-making have a number of processes in common, like roasting, fermenting, seeking out ingredients of the highest quality, and sustainability considerations. A good concept was born. Bit by bit, I tried new things, and over the years I gathered so many ideas and recipes for chocolate and beer that the time had come to put them all together in a book.

My mission in writing this book is to inspire all passionate bakers, pastry chefs, chocolatiers, and chefs who like to work with chocolate and beer. I hope one day I will find this book, dog-eared and stained, in a kitchen or in a chocolate atelier, when I will know that it had an impact and did not just collect dust on a shelf full of other unused cookbooks.

Please enjoy exploring all these creative recipes!

With my utmost gratitude,

Michel Eyckerman,
Technical Advisor for Belcolade
(a division of the Puratos Group)

Belgium is a country that can rightfully be proud of its local products. Our beers and chocolates are praised worldwide for their exceptional quality. This quality is often taken for granted, but it certainly shouldn't be. It is the result of craftsmanship and a relentless pursuit of perfection.

Beer is also gaining increasing recognition in the world of gastronomy — and with good reason. With a broader spectrum of aromas and flavors than wine, beer is exceptionally well-suited to accompany a wide range of dishes. The results are often surprising and innovative.

In this beautiful book, you will discover pairings with some of my favorite beers, such as Cornet and Rodenbach. These beers offer unique taste experiences that pair perfectly with various culinary creations.

I wish you lots of enjoyment while reading — and especially while tasting!

VIKI GEUNES***
Restaurant Zilte
Antwerp (Belgium)

As a chocolatier, I'm always searching for new flavor combinations that spark wonder. Beer offers an incredible palette of aromas — from hoppy bitterness to fruity acidity — that can blend beautifully with the complexity of single-origin chocolate.

In my atelier, for example, we pair pralines with dark Trappist ales, where the caramel notes of the beer enhance the intensity of dark origin chocolate. Or we infuse a fresh IPA into a white chocolate ganache with citrus accents.

For pastry chefs, chocolatiers, and cooks, this book is a playground of creativity. Let your senses guide you, dare to experiment — and above all, enjoy the adventure.

With culinary regards,

Dominique Persoone
Master Chocolatier
The Chocolate Line, Bruges (Belgium)

From taste to technique
How to taste chocolate - Taste descriptions 8
How to taste beer - Taste descriptions 28
How to combine Chocolate & Beer 36
Allergens 38
Decoration tools 43
Tempering chocolate 44
The basics of making molded and colored pralines 48

Decorations **52**

WHAT'S ON THE MENU?

BREAD 'N SPREAD **69**
Chocoladewafel van zuurdesem met tijm 70
Geüpcycled bierbrood met chocoladepasta 73
Chocoladegrissini 74

PREDINNER PLEASURES **77**
Chia parmesan chocolate thins 79
Salty chocolate ribbed chips 80
Blue cheese millefeuille 83
Salty apero bonbons 84
Choux stick chocolate beer dip 86

TASTE TEASERS **89**
Chocolate vinaigrette 91
Brie croquette and chocolate mayo 92
Spiced chocolate rasp and cod 95

MAINS **97**
Beernaise steak and shoestring fries 98
Bacon onion melt bonbon 101

SIGNATURE DESSERTS **105**
Bababeer chocolate chantilly 106
Coco IPA beer dessert exotique 108
Grapefruit IPA raspberry delight 112
Chocolate tripel hoppy 115
Chocolate beer glass dessert 118
Gluten-free moelleux 121

Lactose-free pre-dessert lychee beer sorbet	124
Plant-based banabeer hazelnut	127
Dame Beer Blanche	130
Cherry beer chocolate cake	133
SWEET RETREAT	**137**
Beer churros and chocolate dip	139
Chocolate choux beer and crumble	140
Upcycled anise ganache cookie	142
Beer cake and chocolate	145
Brussels chocolate beer waffle	146
Chocolate beer brownie	149
Amber blondie beer caramel	150
BEER BONBON BOUTIQUE	**153**
Bouchée René Coriander praliné	154
Guinness mallow hops ganache	156
Ultimate beer bottle bonbon	158
Crystal beer syrup bonbon	161
Cherry beer chocolate ganache	162
Amber full beer caramel	165
Chocolate beer orangettes	166
BONBON BEER PAIRINGS	**169**
Pesto salty lemon	171
Tomato lemon pistachio	172
Amber soy sauce speculoos	174
Goat cheese	177
Horseradish beetroot	178
Peanut olive oil and rosemary	181
Smoked bell pepper and spicy almond ravioli	182
Cassis and thyme	185
Crispy Vietnam Clove mandarin	186
Chocolate rosemary lollipops	189
Kadayif pistachio bar	190
CHEERS & CHILLERS	**196**
Hot and cold chocolate cherry beer drink	194
Cocoa beer frappé	197
Acknowledgements	**199**
Colophon	**200**
Conversion Table	**201**

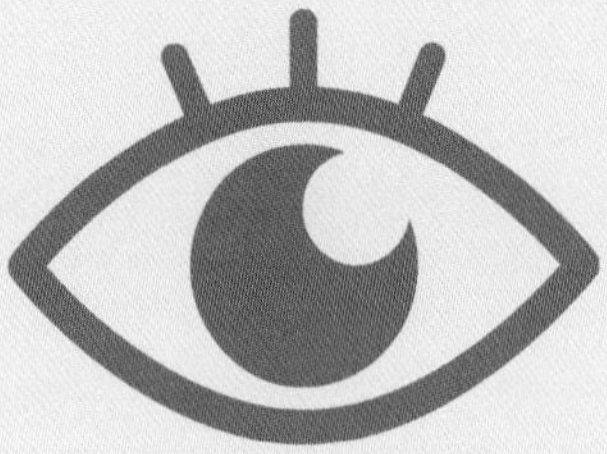

ASPECT

TOUCH

SMELL

Touch

- Wash your hands with unscented soap and rinse them with water.
- Make sure the temperature of the chocolate is around 20 °C.
- Take a piece of chocolate and press it between two fingers to check the melting behavior.
- Break the chocolate and listen to the snap.

Aspect

- Check the color of the chocolate and the shine.
- A well-tempered chocolate exhibits an even color and is required to evaluate the taste & aroma.
- The higher cocoa content of a dark chocolate will give it a darker color.

Smell

- Smell the chocolate and think about all the aromas it might have. Take some time and focus on it.
- For this, it's a good idea to divide the aromas into different categories and then subcategories:
  > **Sweet:** vanilla, caramel
  > **Brown notes:** hazelnut, coffee, almond
  > **Floral:** flower, honey
  > **Vegetal:** humus, wood, fresh grass
  > **Fruity:** banana, dried fruits, olive, citrus, raisin, red berries, pineapple
  > **Cocoa:** acidic, roasted
  > **Dairy:** cooked milk, fresh milk
  > **Spice:** anise, licorice, pepper

How to taste chocolate
The chocolate T.A.S.T.E. journey

TASTE

- Put a piece of chocolate in your mouth and close your eyes.
- Move the chocolate slowly against your palate and let it melt.
- Discover the taste of sweetness, sourness and bitterness in combination with the aromas.

EXPERIENCE

- The chocolate now gives you an unforgettable experience.
- It will take you on a journey of sweetness in combination with bitterness and different aromas.

NOTE ⟶ Certain people are born with a talent for taste and smell, and those people are preordained to be tasting experts. However, even if you're not one of those people, you can still learn how to taste in the best possible way.
First, your nose needs to be clear, so obviously if you've caught a cold it's not the best moment to taste because your nose is probably congested. Also, the best moment of the day to taste is around 11 o'clock in the morning. Do it in an area where you can focus, away from distractions and any perfumes or odors.

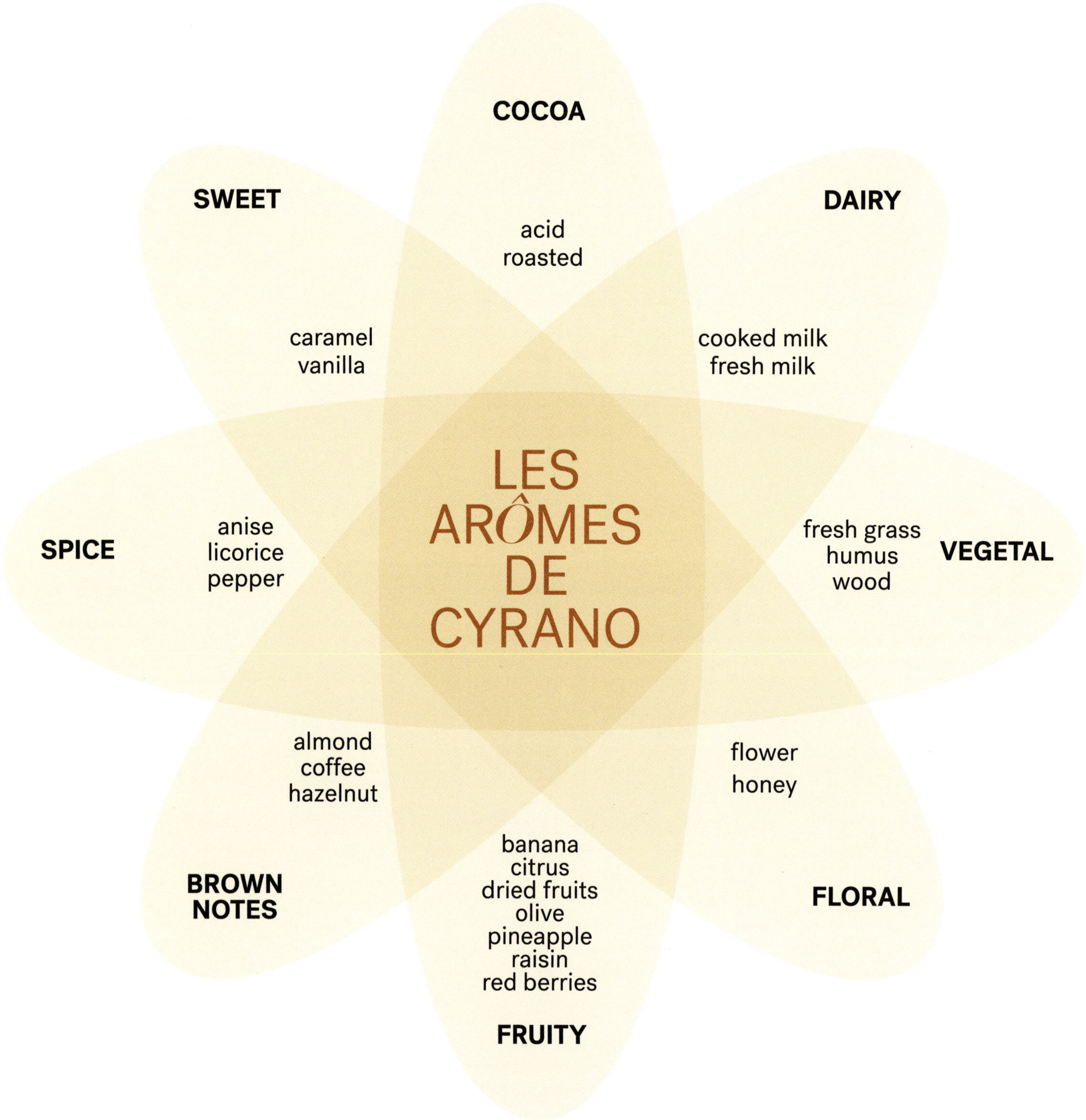
COCOA
acid
roasted
SWEET
caramel
vanilla
DAIRY
cooked milk
fresh milk
SPICE
anise
licorice
pepper
LES ARÔMES DE CYRANO
fresh grass
humus
wood
VEGETAL
almond
coffee
hazelnut
flower
honey
BROWN NOTES
banana
citrus
dried fruits
olive
pineapple
raisin
red berries
FLORAL
FRUITY

TASTE EXPERTISE

The Sensory Map “les Arômes de Cyrano” from Belcolade creates a clear and common understanding of each aroma, so that we can partner them as we work towards crafting the innovative and delicious creations you have in mind.

Knowing which aromas are present in each chocolate is the basis for selecting complementary ingredients.

ORIGINS

Cocoa trees grow within 20° of the equator, thriving in warm temperatures between 21-32 °C, high humidity, and steady rainfall. Tiny midges pollinate their delicate flowers, enabling pod growth — without them, there would be no chocolate. But flavor also depends on terroir: the environment, soil, and even airborne microbes. These factors shape the taste of cocoa beans, giving rise to "single origin" chocolates with unique profiles. For example, Uganda cocoa is bold and earthy, while Ecuadorian beans are floral and fruity. Soil minerals, local vegetation, and fermentation microbes all influence flavor. That's why cocoa from different regions — even under similar climates — tastes distinct. The equator provides the right conditions, but it's the local ecosystem, the farmer, and the fermentation process that give each cocoa its signature character.

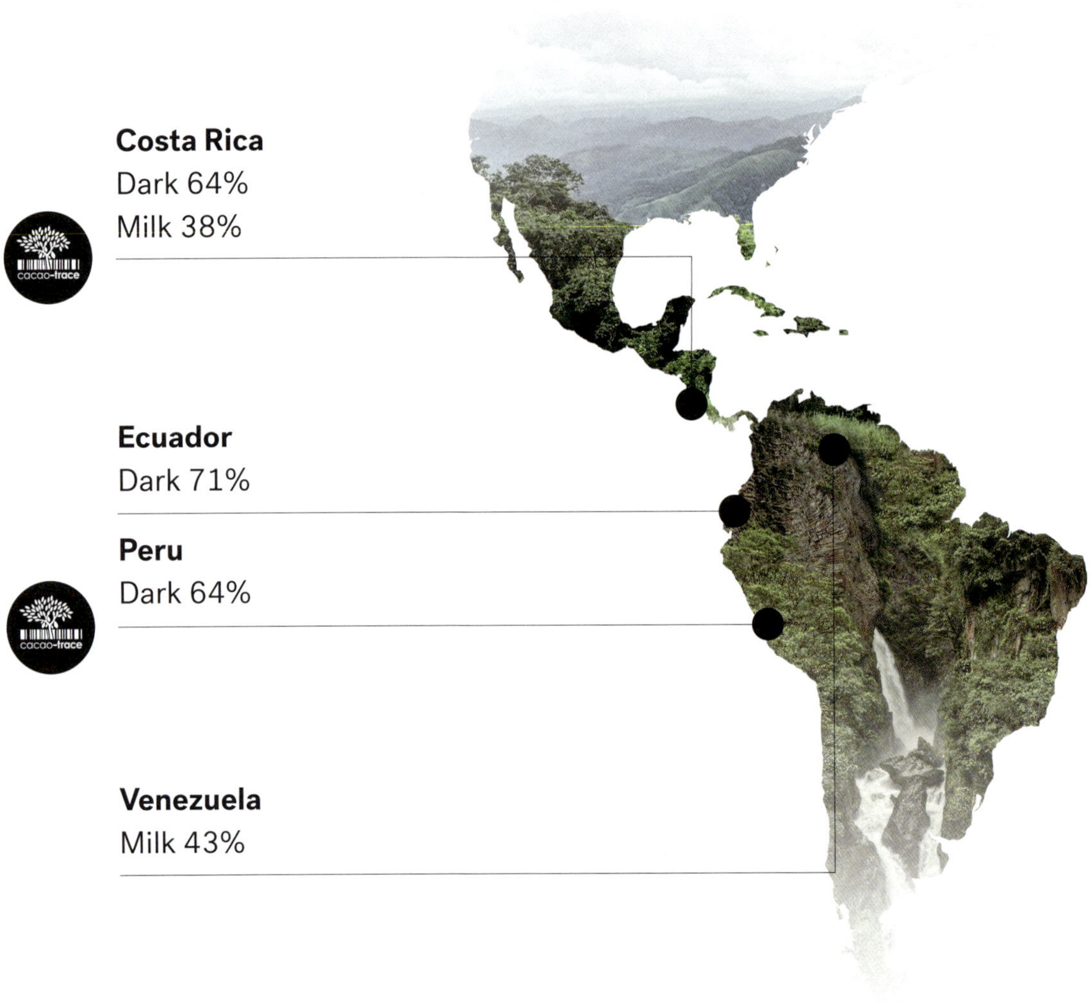

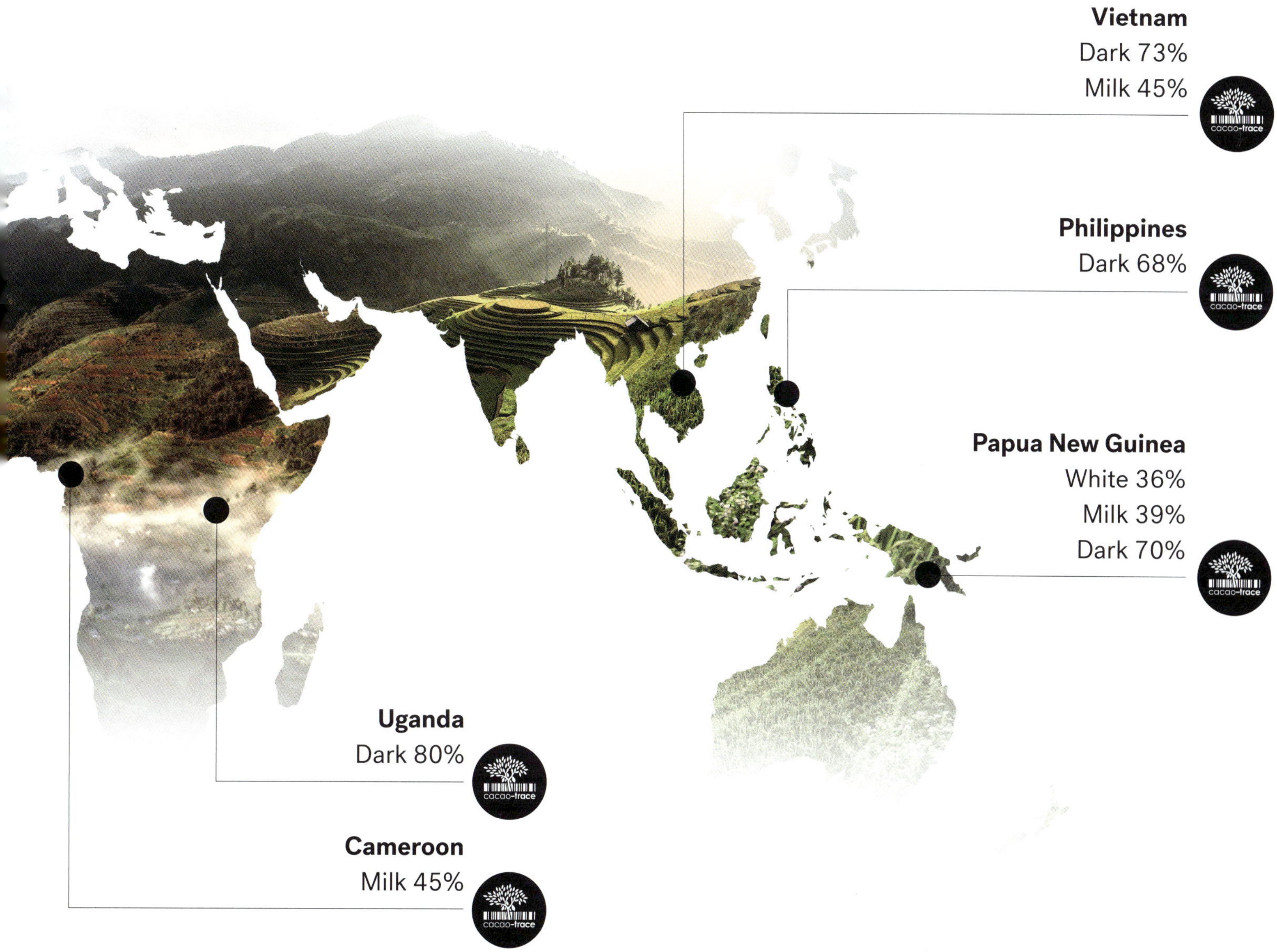
Vietnam
Dark 73%
Milk 45%
Philippines
Dark 68%
Papua New Guinea
White 36%
Milk 39%
Dark 70%
Uganda
Dark 80%
Cameroon
Milk 45%
cacao-trace

CACAO-TRACE: GREAT TASTE, DOING GOOD

As a chocolatier, I care deeply about the planet and the people who grow the cocoa beans. That's why I use sustainable chocolate in my creations both in this book and in my daily practice. It's not just a choice, it's a reflection of my values and dedication to making delicious confectionery that's good for the planet, good for the people, and good for the palate.
By choosing Cacao-Trace chocolate, I'm ensuring that my ingredients come from a program dedicated to improving the lives of cocoa farmers and protecting the environment.

The Cacao-Trace Sustainable Cocoa Program draws on unique expertise in fermentation to bring out exceptional flavors, ensuring that chocolate creations stand out in taste and quality. And by promoting prosperity and fairness throughout our supply chain, this program also ensures that cocoa farmers benefit from the value they create.

This commitment to sustainability includes providing a Quality Premium and a Chocolate Bonus to the Cacao-Trace farmers. These initiatives reward farmers for delivering better-quality cocoa, ensuring they benefit directly.
This leads to better income for cocoa farmers and supports life-changing community projects, such as building schools, maternity wards, and water wells in Cacao-Trace communities.

Join us in building a truly sustainable future for the cocoa industry and everyone involved.

Learn more about Cacao-Trace on
www.cacaotrace.com

GREAT TASTE
DOING GOOD

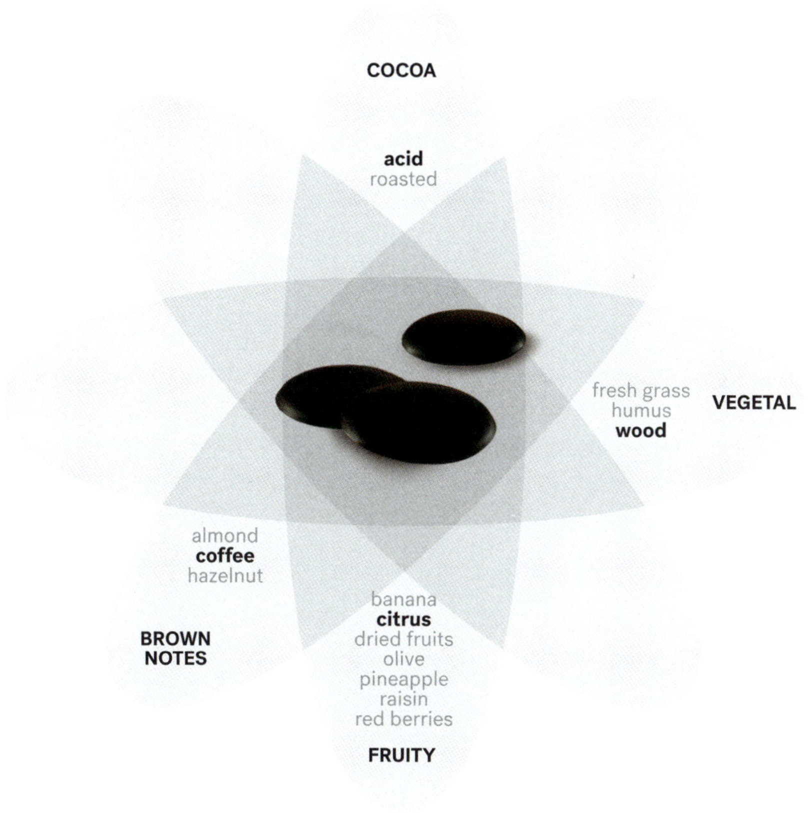

BELCOLADE ORIGINS

Dark Vietnam 73% Cacao-Trace

The Belcolade Origins Dark Vietnam 73% Cacao-Trace is a dark chocolate that overwhelms the senses with the pronounced acidic taste of the Trinitario cocoa bean, zesty citrus notes, light coffee and warm undertones of wood. Guaranteed by the Cacao-Trace experts in Bến Tre.

← *The main varieties of cocoa are Criollo, Forastero, Trinitario and Nacional, each with their unique flavors.*

BELCOLADE ORIGINS

Milk Vietnam 45% Cacao-Trace

This heavenly flavor combination of Asia's "little Venice" has been cultivated and safeguarded by the Cacao-Trace farmers. The Belcolade Origins Milk Vietnam 45% Cacao-Trace is a milk chocolate containing a subtle mix of caramel & coffee with a touch of roasted cocoa bean flavor.

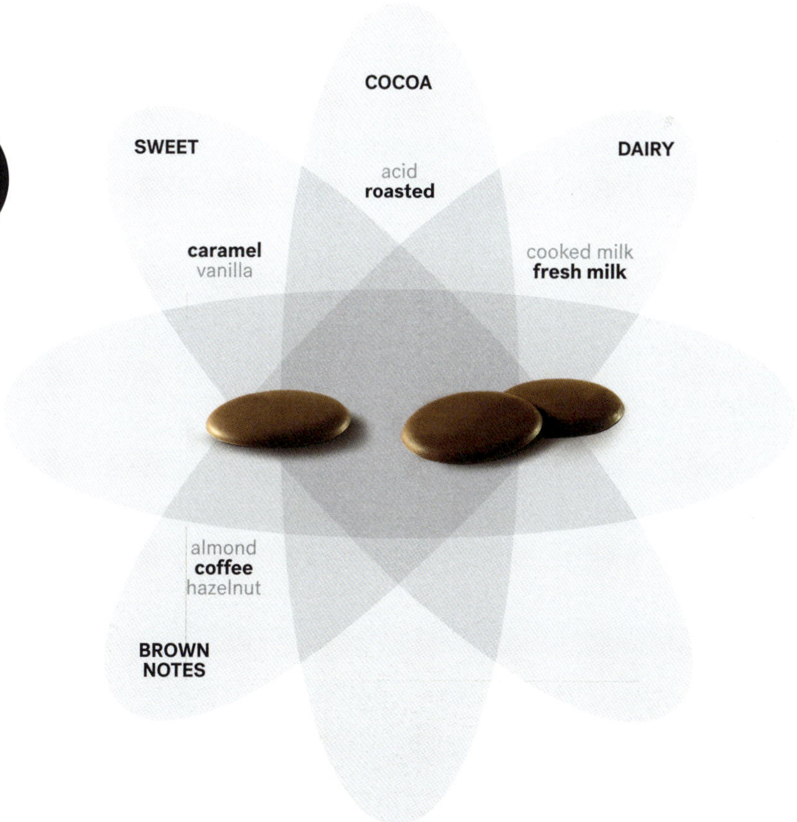

↑ *Cocoa trees generally grow in tropical regions with high humidity, consistent rainfall and warm temperatures.*

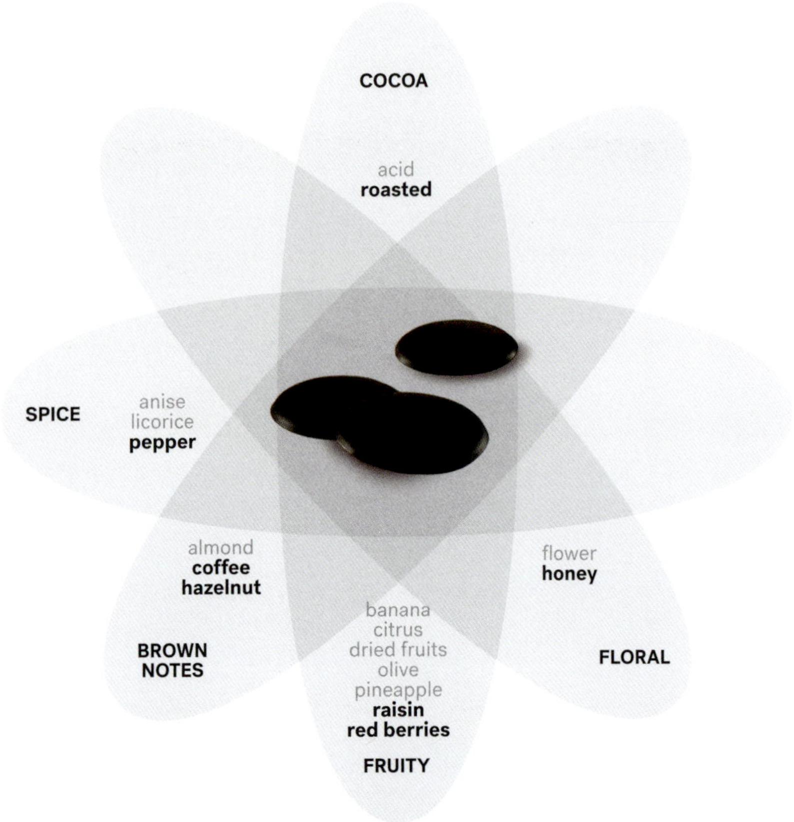

BELCOLADE ORIGINS

Dark Papua New Guinea 70% Organic Cacao-Trace

The surprising complexity of flavors makes this organic chocolate delightfully special. Based on pure, roasted cocoa, this unique chocolate combines the roasted flavors of coffee and hazelnut with notes of both fresh and dried fruit. And there's more: underlying hints of black pepper and honey.

Milk Papua New Guinea 39% Organic Cacao-Trace

With a cocoa content of 39%, this very fresh and creamy organic milk chocolate crafted from the most flavorful beans offers a characteristic caramel flavor with underlying notes of fruits and a touch of hazelnut.

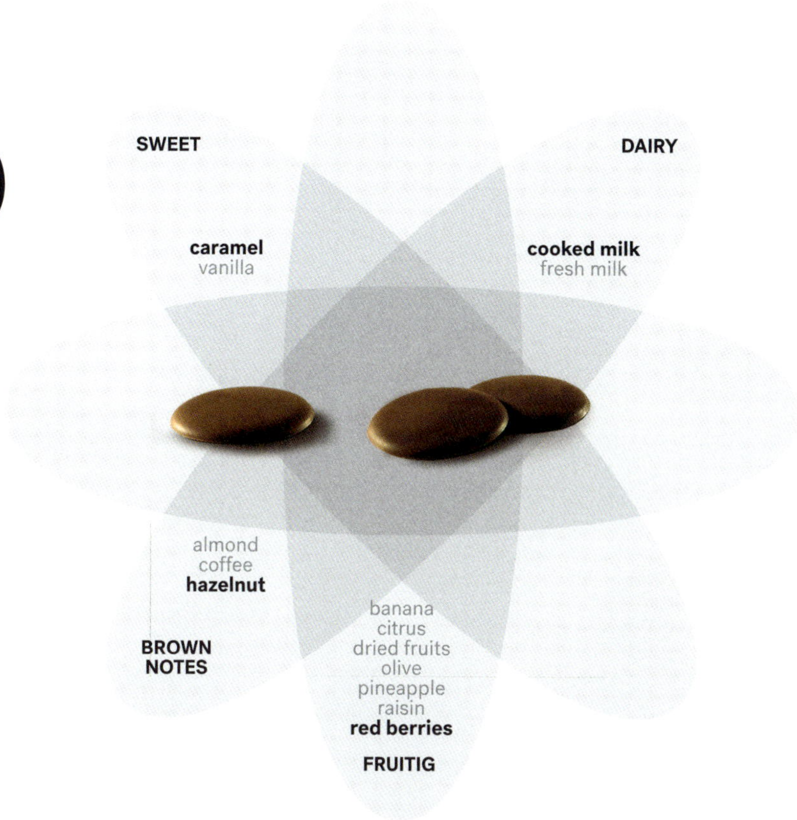

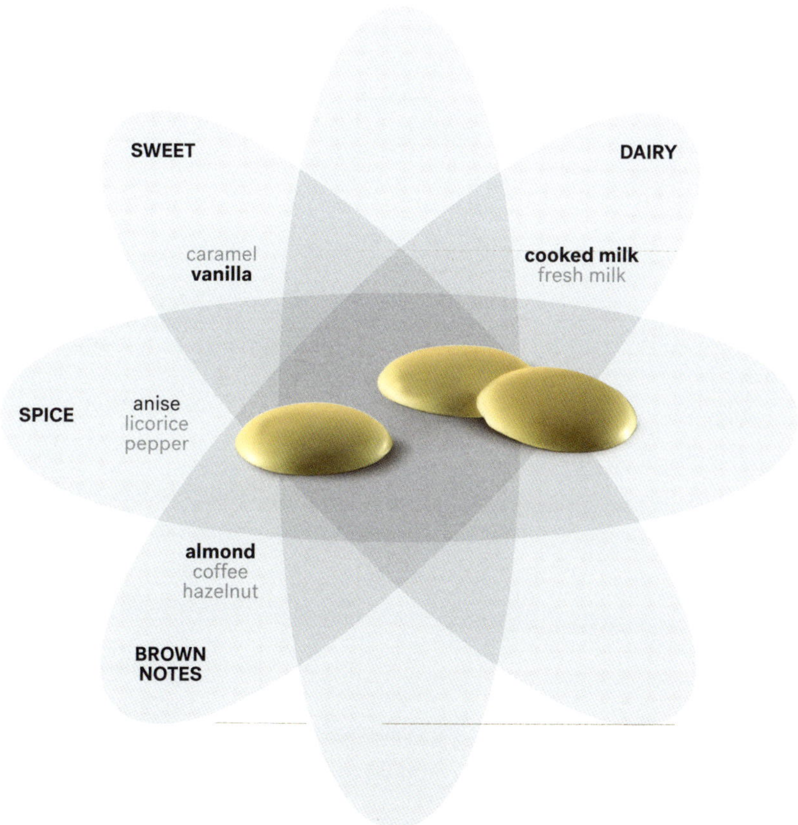

BELCOLADE ORIGINS

White Papua New Guinea 36% Cacao-Trace

An amazing single-origin white chocolate made with Papua New Guinea vanilla, which unveils rich notes of coumarin, peach and balsamic notes. This complex vanilla flavor meets intense cooked milk and buttery notes. Undertones of almond and anise softly round out this unique taste experience.

↑ *Cacao tree flowers are small, pinkish-white, grow on trunks and branches, and require pollination.*

BELCOLADE ORIGINS

Dark Philippines 68% Cacao-Trace

This dark chocolate gives a delightful blend of fruity notes, with dominating flavors of tropical fruits such as pineapple, banana and passion fruit, complemented by notes of red and dried fruits. The flavor profile is further enhanced by fresh grass and floral notes, highlighted by a touch of pepper.

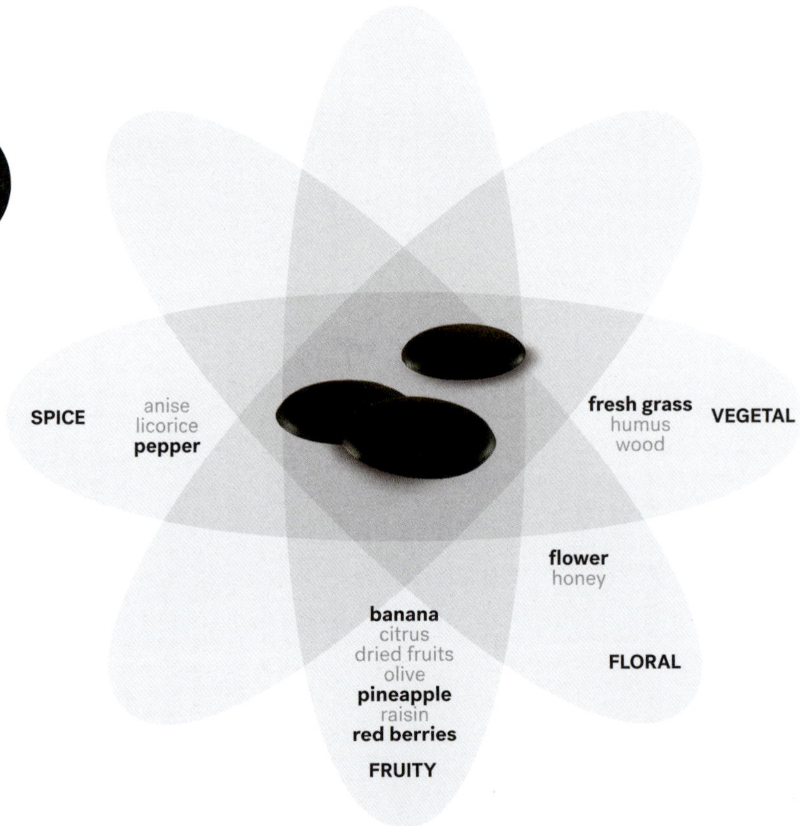

↑ *On a plantation, a farmer can harvest up to 1,000 cocoa pods per day, depending on the conditions.*

BELCOLADE ORIGINS

Dark Uganda 80% Organic Cacao-Trace

Product of the mineral-rich soil of the Bundibugyo region and the craftsmanship of local organic farmers, this dark chocolate offers a deep and long-lasting roasted cocoa intensity. Cacao-Trace guaranteed, the robust cocoa flavor is delicately enriched by delightful fresh citrusy & dried fruit notes, while unveiling subtle earthy notes of humus and loam.

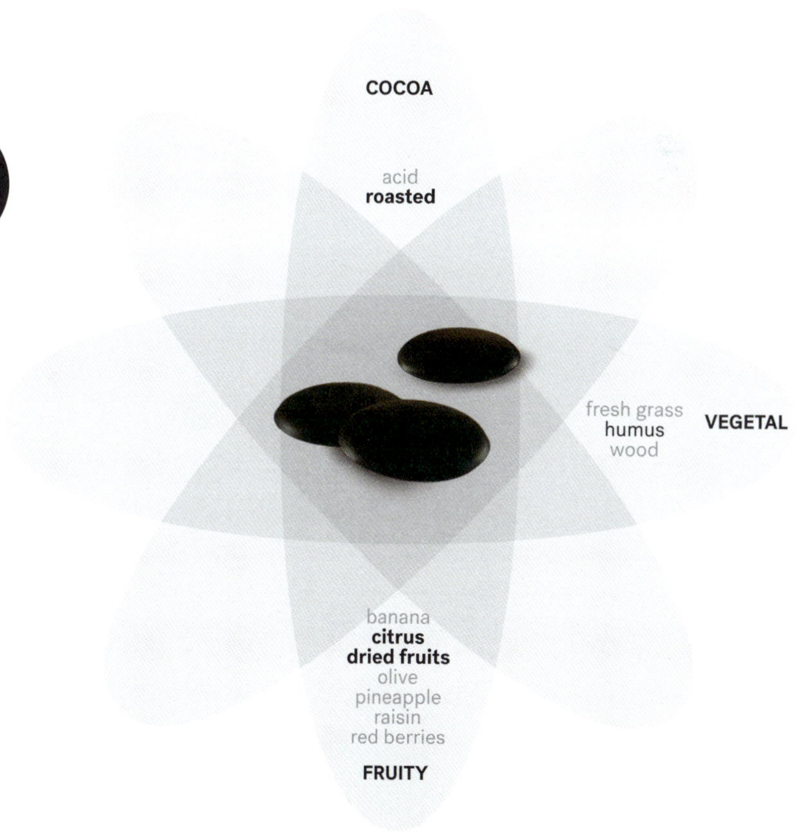

↑ *The opening of the pods is done manually with a machete. Each pod contains between 20 and 50 beans.*

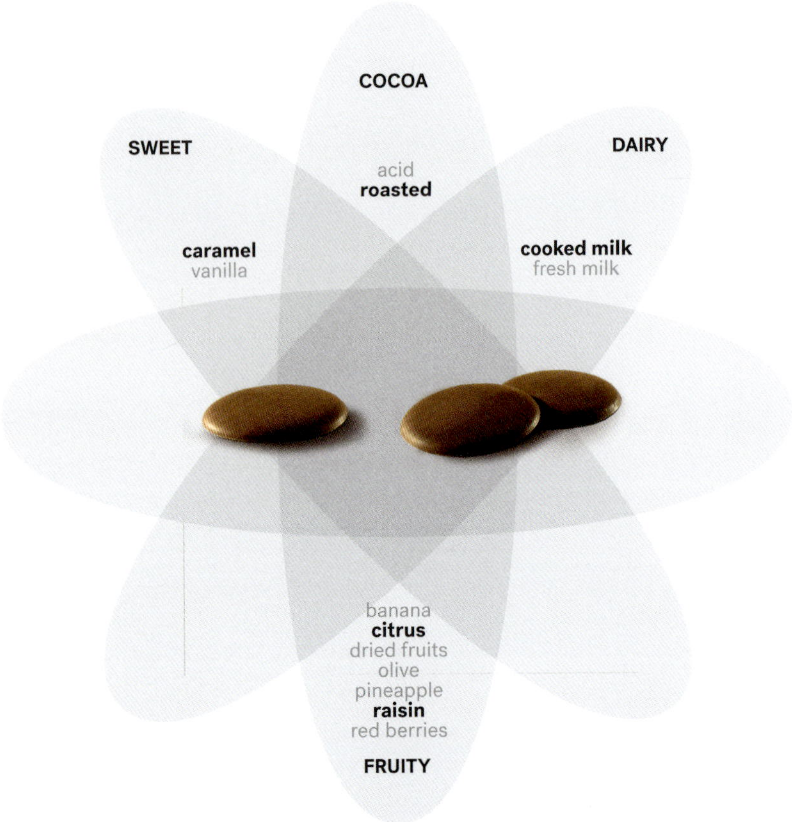

BELCOLADE ORIGINS

Milk Cameroon 45% Cacao-Trace

Born from the lush soil of the valleys of the Sanaga river, the red Trinitario beans are characteristic of the high-quality standards of Cacao-Trace. Meet the result: this surprisingly intense milk chocolate, which offers deep roasted cocoa notes finely balanced by cooked milk and caramel flavors, ending on a delicate touch of dried fruits.

↑ *The fermentation process is very crucial for the development of a quality cocoa flavor of the final chocolate; this takes 5 to 7 days.*

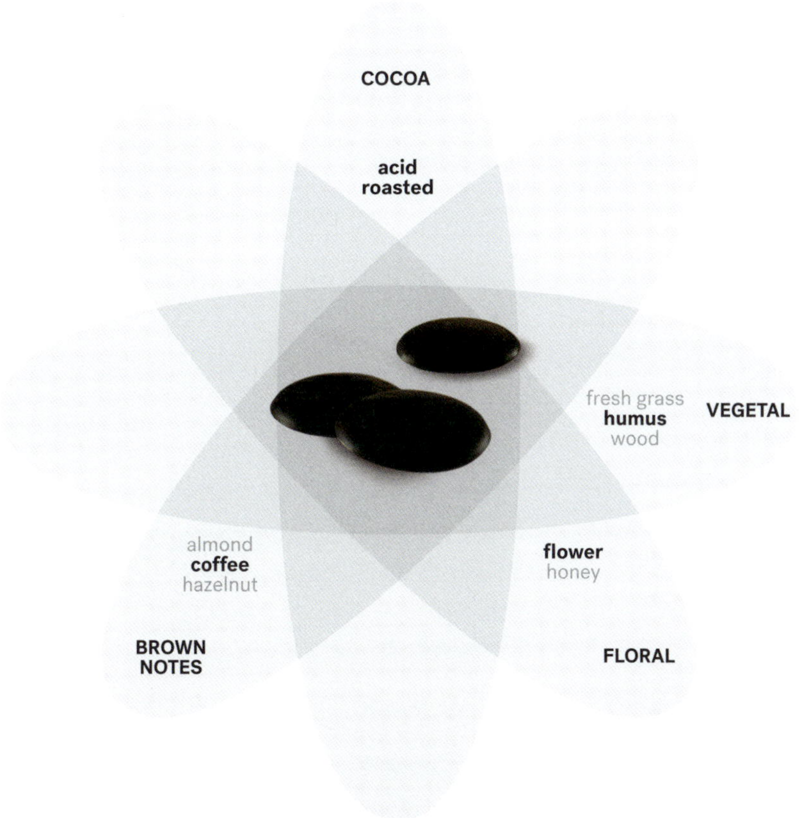

BELCOLADE ORIGINS

Dark Ecuador 71%

Be exhilarated by the luscious floral bouquet of Belcolade Origins Dark Ecuador 71%, a dark chocolate made from Nacional cocoa beans that bursts with character and flavor. Its delicate notes of jasmine are complemented by the appealing touch of coffee and humus. It is a match made in heaven, but cultivated in the fertile soils of the Esmeraldas and Los Rios regions.

Quality cocoa beans are sun-dried on open air beds to reduce moisture and prevent spoilage.

BELCOLADE ORIGINS

Dark Peru 64% Cacao-Trace

For a totally irresistible dark chocolate, try Belcolade Origins Dark Peru 64%. No other chocolate so successfully and delightfully unites the enticing flavors of Peru's rich cocoa farming heritage and the Amazon's primeval wilderness. By mixing Criollo and Trinitario cocoa beans, a dark chocolate like no other has been created, with a slightly acidic cocoa taste enhanced with notes of raisins and dried figs. Once tasted, never forgotten.

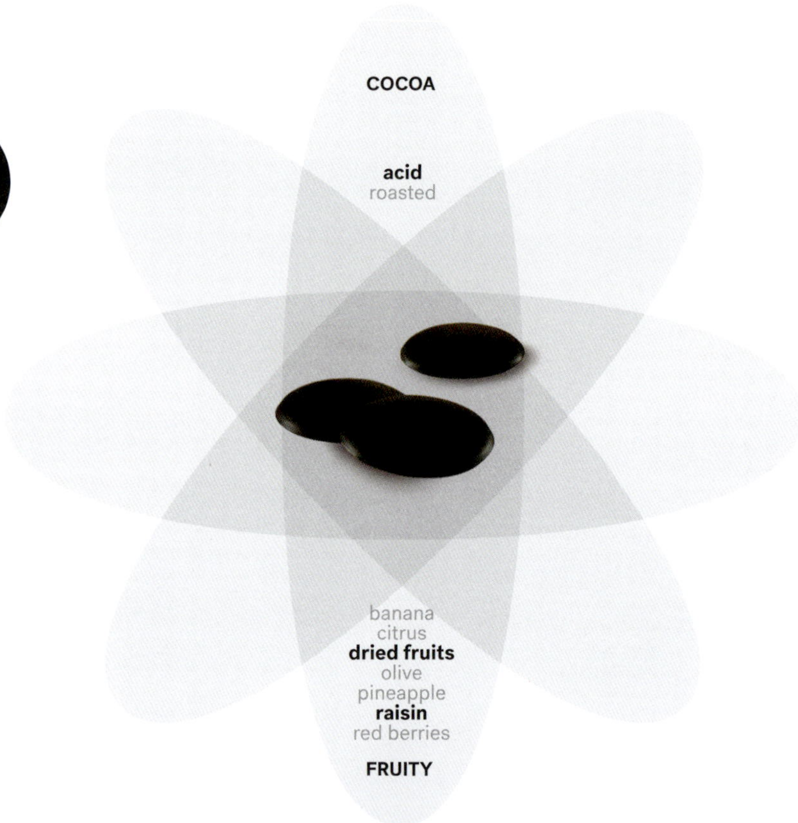

↑ *The cocoa beans are packed in jute sacks and stored in a clean, dry and sterile place out of the sun.*

BELCOLADE ORIGINS

Milk Venezuela 43%

This divine milk chocolate entices and then delights, thanks to its luscious nutty base and classic "chocolatey" notes. These Criollo cocoa beans result in a strong flavor of caramel, hazelnuts and cooked milk with a hint of roasted cocoa. Crafted with care, this rich, warm combination draws you back to the roots of taste, to the heat of Venezuela and the heart of the Amazon.

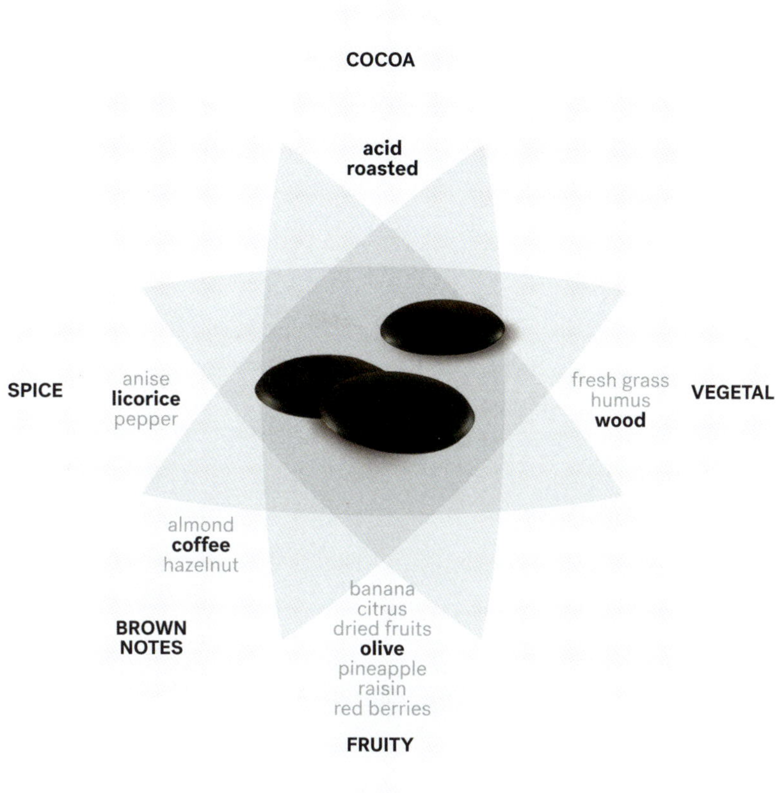

BELCOLADE ORIGINS

Dark Costa Rica 64% Cacao-Trace

The ideal climate and soil conditions of Costa Rica, combined with the craftsmanship of local farmers and taste experts, create this traditional, smooth dark chocolate made from Trinitario beans. Savor the complex medley of wood and olive, which mingles with the enticing aromas of coffee and licorice and a magical hint of acidic roasted cocoa in the background.

← *The cocoa beans are now ready to be shipped to chocolate producing facilities.*

BELCOLADE ORIGINS

Milk Costa Rica 38% Cacao-Trace

With a cocoa content of 38%, this mild chocolate is crafted from Trinitario cocoa beans lovingly grown and expertly harvested by local farmers. Discover the aromas of cooked milk and a touch of vanilla resulting in a velvety smooth eating experience. Every bite is pure delight.

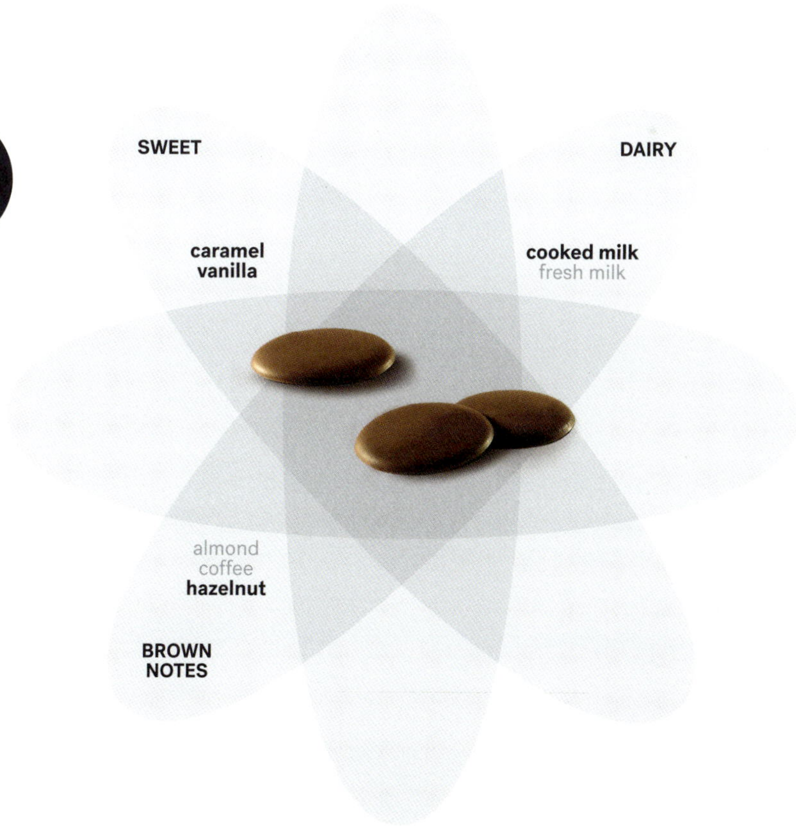

TOUCH

- Normally, the serving temperature of the beer will be indicated on the bottle. Touch the bottle to verify the temperature.

- Beer should also be stored in a cool, dark place away from sunlight to avoid oxidation of the flavors.

ASPECT

- The first step is to make sure the beer glass is clean and appealing. The best glass for a beer tasting session is comparable to a wine glass. With this type of glass the aromas stay in the glass longer.

- Pour out the beer and check the foam for color, density and cling.

- Visually check the beer's color, transparency and bubbles.

SMELL

- Smell the aromas coming off the foam.

- **Hoppiness:** Hops contribute bitterness and can add floral, citrus, pine or herbal notes. These aromas are prominent in beers like IPAs and pale ales.

- **Fruity esters:** These are produced by yeast during fermentation and can give off fruity aromas such as banana, pear or apple. These are common in ales and wheat beers.

- **Maltiness:** This can include sweet, bready and caramel notes. Malt aromas are often associated with flavors like toast, nuts and chocolate, especially in darker beers like porters and stouts.

- **Spices:** Some beers have spicy notes like clove, pepper or coriander. These can come from specific yeast strains or added spices, often found in Belgian-style beers.

- Also be alert to off-flavors like dimethyl sulphide, broccoli, garlic aromas, chewing gum flavor, etc.

How to taste beer

The beer T.A.S.T.E. journey

TASTE

EXPERIENCE

- Taste the beer but leave it in your mouth for 3 seconds before swallowing it.
- You will find the sourness and the sweetness first, and then, when you swallow the beer, you will taste the bitterness more in the back of the mouth.

- Discover the aromas in the retronasal phase.
- Experience the mouthfeel and the aftertaste.
- At this point you'll have the after-aromas of the beer, like the bitter flavors of the hops, that linger in your mouth longer.
- Now you'll experience a rising, astringent bitterness that makes you feel like drinking more beer. Be aware of it and drink in moderation.

Beer descriptions

Knowing the flavor profiles of the beer is crucial for creating a harmonious pairing with chocolate. Here you can find some information and explanation on the flavor, strength, taste and color of the beers I use. Good to know is the IBU, EBC and the ABV of the beers.

IBU

International Bitterness Units
Measures the bitterness of the beer

IBU is a scale used to measure the bitterness of beer. The bitterness primarily comes from the hops used during brewing. The higher the IBU value, the more bitter the beer will taste.

Why It Matters

- **Strength Bitterness:** Higher IBU values indicate more bitterness, which can significantly influence the taste of the beer. Bitterness can balance out sweetness and add complexity to the flavor profile.

IBU Scale

0-10	**IBU**	Very low bitterness (e.g., Light Lagers, Wheat Beers)
10-20	**IBU**	Low bitterness (e.g., Pilsners, Blonde Ales)
20-35	**IBU**	Moderate bitterness (e.g., Pale Ales, Amber Ales)
35-50	**IBU**	High bitterness (e.g., IPAs, American Pale Ales)
50+	**IBU**	Very high bitterness (e.g., Double IPAs, Imperial IPAs)

EBC

European Brewery Convention
Measures the color of the beer

EBC is a standard for measuring the color of beer. It quantifies the color intensity of the beer, with higher EBC values indicating darker beers. The measurement is done using a spectrophotometer, which assesses how much light is absorbed by the beer at a specific wavelength.

Why It Matters

- **Flavor:** Darker beers (higher EBC) often have richer, more malty flavors, while lighter beers (lower EBC) tend to have lighter, crisper flavors. However, this is a generalization and there are exceptions.

EBC (Color) Scale

0-4	**EBC**	Pale Straw
4-8	**EBC**	Pale Gold
8-12	**EBC**	Deep Gold
12-20	**EBC**	Amber
20-30	**EBC**	Deep Amber
30-40	**EBC**	Copper
40-60	**EBC**	Brown
60-80	**EBC**	Dark Brown
80+	**EBC**	Black

COLOUR														
EBC	4	6	8	12	16	20	26	33	39	47	57	69	79	139
POSSIBLE BEER STYLES	Pale Lager	Golden Ale	Weiss	APA, IPA	Saison	ESB	Garde (Bière de Garde), DIPA (Double IPA)	Amber Ale	Dunkel, Brown Ale	Porter	Stout	Baltic Porter	Export Stout	Imp. Stout

ABV

Alcohol By Volume

Indicates the amount of alcohol by volume

Why It Matters

- **Strength:** Higher ABV beers are stronger and can have a more pronounced effect.
- **Flavor:** The alcohol content can influence the flavor profile of the beer. Higher ABV beers often have richer, more complex flavors.
- **Calories:** Beers with higher ABV typically contain more calories.

Alcohol Content Scale for Beers

3-4% ABV	Light Beers (e.g., Light Lagers, Session Ales)
4-6% ABV	Regular Beers (e.g., Pale Ales, Pilsners, Amber Ales)
6-7% ABV	Strong Beers (e.g., IPAs, Belgian Ales)
7-12% ABV	Very Strong Beers (e.g., Double IPAs, Imperial Stouts, Barleywines)
12%+ ABV	Extremely Strong Beers (e.g., Strong Ales, some specialty craft brews)

Different beer styles

organized from lowest to highest EBC

Pale Lager (EBC 2-6)
- **Description:** Light, crisp, and refreshing. Often has mild flavors and low bitterness.
- **Example:** Bavik Super Pils

Wheat Beer (EBC 4-8)
- **Description:** Light and cloudy with a smooth, creamy texture. Often has fruity and spicy notes.
- **Example:** Hoegaarden White

Pilsner (EBC 6-12)
- **Description:** Pale gold with a crisp, clean taste. Typically has a noticeable hop bitterness.
- **Example:** Jupiler, Stella Artois, Maes Pils

Blonde Ale (EBC 6-12)
- **Description:** Light and easy-drinking with mild malt sweetness and low bitterness.
- **Example:** Kwaremont

Pale Ale (EBC 8-14)
- **Description:** Amber to deep gold with a balanced malt and hop profile. Often has fruity and floral notes.
- **Example:** Orval

Amber Ale (EBC 12-20)
- **Description:** Amber to copper with a rich malt character and moderate hop bitterness.
- **Example:** Dobbel PALM

IPA (India Pale Ale) (EBC 10-20)
- **Description:** Amber to copper with strong hop bitterness and aromatic flavors. Can range from fruity to piney.
- **Example:** Duvel Tripel Hop Citra

Brown Ale (EBC 20-40)
- **Description:** Dark amber to brown with a malty sweetness and nutty, caramel flavors.
- **Example:** Leffe Brune, Rochefort 8

Porter (EBC 30-60)
- **Description:** Dark brown to black with roasted malt flavors, often including chocolate and coffee notes.
- **Example:** Lupulus Hibernatus

Stout (EBC 40-80)
- **Description:** Very dark brown to black with rich, roasted flavors. Can include notes of coffee, chocolate, and caramel.
- **Example:** Guinness

Imperial Stout (EBC 60-100+)
- **Description:** Black with intense roasted malt flavors and higher alcohol content. Often has complex flavors including dark fruits and chocolate.
- **Example:** Troubadour Imperial Stout

Beer styles used in this recipe book

Belgian Pale Ale

- **Bolleke De Koninck (EBC 30, IBU 23, 5,2%, 8-10 °C):** Spéciale Belge, slightly malty with hoppy hints, caramel notes and toasted bread.
- **Grandgousier (EBC 7, IBU 35, 5%, 6-8°C):** A Belgian pale ale with a refreshing complex aroma, green and hoppy with fruity and floral notes.

Belgian Trappist ale

- **Orval (EBC 18, IBU 36, 6,2%, 10-15°C):** A Belgian Trappist ale. Complex, fruity, and slightly bitter with a dry finish. Notes of citrus, spice, and earthy hops.

Witbier

- **Hoegaarden White (EBC 5, IBU 15, 4,9%, 4-6°C):** Light, fruity, and refreshing with hints of citrus and coriander. Notes of orange peel and wheat.
- **Vedett Extra White (EBC 4, IBU 15, 4,7%, 4-6°C):** A wheat beer, refreshing with citrus, honey and coriander flavors.
- **Blanche De Namur (EBC 5, IBU 10, 4,5%, 4-6°C):** Smooth mellow notes of citrus and coriander, hints of orange peel and wheat.

Pilsner

- **Bavik Super Pils (EBC 6, IBU 21, 5,2%, 4-6°C):** Crisp, clean, and refreshing with a mild bitterness. Light malt sweetness and herbal hop character.

Belgian Blond Ale

- **Kwaremont (EBC 14, IBU 28, 6,6%, 6-10°C):** Balanced Belgian blond ale, malty and slightly bitter, with a smooth finish. Flavors of caramel and herbal hops.
- **Omer Blond (EBC 7, IBU 30, 8%, 6-8°C):** Balanced, fruity, and slightly bitter with a smooth finish. Flavors of pear, apple, and malt.

Belgian Strong Pale Ale

- **Kwak Blonde (EBC 12, IBU 20, 7,4%, 4-6°C):** Fruity, malty and slightly sweet smooth finish. Notes of banana and caramel.
- **Delirium Tremens (EBC 7,5, IBU 24,5, 8,5%, 8-10°C):** Fruity, slightly sweet with a dry finish. Aromas of apple, pear and spice.

Belgian Dark Strong Ale

- **Lupulus Hibernatus (EBC 112, IBU 30, 9,5%, 8-12°C):** Rich, dark and malty with notes of chocolate and coffee. Hints of dark fruit and roasted barley.
- **Gouden Carolus Whiskey Infused (EBC 70, IBU 15, 11,7%, 10-12°C):** A dark ale that's smooth, rich, and warming with hints of whiskey. Flavors of caramel, vanilla, and oak.
- **Carolus Imperial Dark (EBC 70, IBU 15, 11%, 10-12°C):** Rich roasted malt flavors complemented with caramel notes and hints of dark fruit.

Tripel

- **Tripel D'Anvers (EBC 9, IBU 16, 8%, 8-10°C):** A strong tripel with fruity, spicy aromas. Slightly sweet with a dry finish. Aromas of banana, clove, and citrus.
- **Tripel Karmeliet (EBC 9, IBU 13, 8,4%, 6-9°C):** A refined tripel with complex, fruity, and spicy aromas. A smooth finish with flavors of banana, vanilla, and clove.
- **Fourchette Beer (EBC 7, IBU 22, 7%, 8-12°C):** A Belgian tripel with balanced, fruity, and slightly bitter aromas. A refreshing finish and notes o fcitrus, spice, and malt.
- **Orvélo Tripel (EBC 15, IBU 30, 7,5%, 6-10°C):** Floral profile with mild spice. Medium-dry citrus bitterness with hints of rosemary and coriander.
- **La Trappe Tripel (EBC 14, IBU 25, 8%, 8-10°C):** Fruity, malty, and slightly sweet with a dry finish. Flavors of apricot, honey, and spice.
- **Westmalle Trappist Tripel (EBC 11, IBU 36, 9,5%, 8-10°C):** A classic tripel with malty, fruity tones. Slightly sweet with a dry finish. Flavors of dark fruit, caramel, and spice.

Belgian Strong Blond Ale

- **Cornet Oaked Strong Blond (EBC 8, IBU 25, 8,5%, 6-7°C):** A strong blond ale with a smooth, oaky flavor and with a slight sweetness. Hints of vanilla with flavors of caramel and toasted malt.
- **Dobbel PALM (EBC 41, IBU 21, 5,7, 4-6°C):** An amber-colored special Belgian ale with pronounced maltiness, caramel notes and hints of toasted bread.

Flemish Red-Brown Ale

- **Rodenbach Classic (EBC 65, IBU 9, 5,2%, 6-8°C):** A sour ale with fruity vinous flavors. Tart, fruity, and refreshing with a balanced sourness. Notes of red berries and oak.
- **Rodenbach Grand Cru (EBC 70, IBU 8, 6%, 4-6°C):** A more intense version of the classic, with deeper sour and fruity notes. Tart, fruity complex balanced by notes of sourness, red berries and oak.

Geuze

- **Oude Geuze Cuvée René (EBC 12, IBU 10, 6%, 6-8°C):** A blend of aged lambics, resulting in a complex sour with a dry finish. Flavors of green apple, berries and lemon.
- **Boon Oude Geuze (EBC 12, IBU 22, 7%, 6-10°C):** A traditional geuze made from a blend of aged lambics, offering a tart and refreshing taste. Complex sourness, funky aromas, and notes of green apple, lemon and barnyard funk.

Irish Dry Stout

- **Guinness Extra Stout (EBC 90, IBU 15, 4,2%, 6-8°C):** A rich and creamy dry stout with notes of coffee and chocolate. Hints of roasted barley and caramel.

Dubbel:

- **Westmalle Trappist Dubbel (EBC 80, IBU 29, 7%, 10-12°C):** Malty, fruity and slightly sweet with a dry finish. Flavors of dark fruit, caramel and spice.
- **Brugse Zot Dubbel (EBC 75, IBU 27, 7,5%, 10-12°C):** Rich and malty, slightly sweet with notes of chocolate and caramel with hints of dark fruit.
- **La Trappe Dubbel (EBC 82, IBU 20, 7%, 10-12°C):** Malty and fruity. Slightly sweet with a dry finish. Flavors of dark fruit, caramel and spice.

Saison

- **Saison Dupont (EBC 11, IBU 27, 6,5%, 8-12°C):** Fruity, spicy and slightly bitter with a refreshing finish. Notes of grapefruit, cloves and malt.
- **Saison De Dottignies (EBC 16, IBU 45, 5,5%, 8-12°C):** Fruity, hoppy, and slightly bitter with a refreshing finish. Notes of citrus, spice, and malt.

Belgian IPA

- **De Ranke XX Bitter (EBC 10, IBU 60, 6%, 8-10°C):** Highly bitter distinct hop flavors, balanced maltiness and notes of citrus and pine.
- **Houblon Chouffe (EBC 10, IBU 52, 9%, 6-10°C):** Fruity characteristics. Pronounced notes of hop bitterness with grapefruit and pine flavors.
- **Duvel Tripel Hop Citra Belgian IPA (EBC 7, IBU 40, 9,5%, 6-8°C):** Intense citrus aromas with a balanced bitterness. Notes of Citra hop, grapefruit and tropical fruits.

Dry beer and alcohol free

- **Brussels Beer Project Pico Bello (EBC 6, IBU 20, 0,3%, 4-6°C):** Fruity aromas with a touch of bitterness. Alcohol-free beer with a refreshing acidity.
- **Deus Brut Des Flandres (EBC 10, IBU 11, 11,5%, 2-4°C):** A delicate pale golden beer combining apple, pear and honey. Spicy flavors with a complex profile and refined bubbles.

IPA

- **Kerel Grapefruit IPA (EBC 23, IBU 53, 5%, 6-8°C):** Bold grapefruit flavor. Tart character with light hoppiness and notes of citrus zest.
- **Vedett IPA (EBC 12, IBU 40, 5,5%, 6-8°C):** A hoppy IPA with balanced bitterness and fruitiness. Citrus notes and hints of caramel. Some floral notes.

Fruit Lambic (Kriek)

- **Lindemans Kriek (EBC 49, IBU 15, 3,5%, 4-6°C):** A lambic with strong cherry flavors. Sweet, fruity, and refreshing with hints of almond and tartness.
- **Timmermans Lambicus Kriek (EBC 20, IBU 10, 4%, 4-6°C):** Sweet cherry flavors combined with a refreshing tartness. Hints of almonds. Wheat beer base.
- **Kriek Mystic (EBC 48, IBU 10, 3,5%, 4-6°C):** Refreshing cherry taste, combined wheat beer base and notes of almonds and tartness.

Flanders Oud Bruin

- **Liefmans Goudenband (EBC 37, IBU 16, 8%, 6-8°C):** Complex, fruity and slightly sour with a rich finish. Notes of red berries and caramelized malt.

Quadrupel

- **St Bernardus Abt 12 (EBC 60, IBU 20, 10%, 10-12°C):** Dark brown color, robust ivory head, complex flavor profile of fruity aromas and a caramel bittersweet finish.

Belgian Strong Dark Ale

- **Chimay Blue (EBC 68, IBU 20, 9%, 10-12°C):** Rich dark fruit flavors complemented with chocolate notes. Hints of caramel and spice.

Flanders Red Ale

- **Rodenbach Caractère Rouge (EBC 22, IBU 8, 7%, 6-8°C):** Complex fruitiness, balanced sourness and notes of red berries with oak.

Stout

- **Kerel Stout (EBC 59, IBU 44, 6%, 10-12°C):** Dark, rich roasted notes. Chocolate and coffee flavors with hints of roasted barley.
- **Monk's Stout Dupont (EBC 118, IBU 27, 5,2%, 10-12°C):** A dark beer with roasted malt flavors. Roasted barley and notes of coffee and chocolate.

Imperial Stout

- **Gulden Draak Imperial Stout (EBC 110, IBU 17, 12%, 10-12°C):** Bold and intense with flavors of chocolate and coffee. Notes of dark fruit and roasted malt.
- **Troubadour Imperial Stout (EBC 110, IBU 45, 9%, 10-12°C):** A dark, intense stout with complex flavors including chocolate and coffee. Roasted malt.

Pairing beer and chocolate works best when you match their intensity and flavor profiles. Dark beers like stouts pair beautifully with bold, earthy dark chocolates, while fruity or spiced ales complement lighter, floral chocolates.
If you don't have access to a specific brand, focus on single origin chocolate. Cocoa beans from the same region — like Peru, Ecuador, or Vietnam — often share similar taste notes due to local soil, climate, and fermentation microbes. Choose chocolate with a similar cocoa percentage and fat content to maintain texture and richness in recipes.
For example, an Ecuadorian 71% chocolate can be replaced with another from the same region and percentage for a close match. Always taste both beer and chocolate together to fine-tune the pairing and highlight their shared flavors.

COMPARE

Compare similar flavors in the chocolate and the beer. A dark semi-sweet chocolate with a roasted, coffee flavor profile could work with a dark stout beer because of the roasted malt used in the brewing process, which gives the beer coffee undertones.

CONTRAST

This method focuses on pairing beer and chocolate with opposing flavors to create a balanced experience. Look for contrasts in flavors: a sweet chocolate works very well with a beer style like Geuze, where you have the contrast of the sweetness from the chocolate and the sourness of the beer.

CLEANSE

This approach uses the beer to cleanse the palate between bites of chocolate. A crisp, refreshing lager beer can cleanse the palate after a bite of rich, creamy chocolate, preparing your taste buds for the next bite.

How to combine Chocolate & Beer

There are a number of options...

COMPLEMENT

As chefs, this is our daily work. After years of experience, we know how to combine flavors into something amazing. For example, when you drink an IPA, eating a fruity chocolate with an acidic cocoa taste profile can boost the taste experience. The acidity of the chocolate makes the fruitiness of the beer come out more.

COMBINE

This book presents all the primary flavor profiles of the beers and chocolates used. Don't be afraid to experiment; there's no "wrong" way to pair beer and chocolate. When you experiment with combinations you will find some pairings that you like better than others. Some combinations might seem "wrong," but even these will bring new and unexpected flavors out of both the chocolate and the beer.

ALLERGENS

This book addresses an important topic: Next to each recipe, we indicate if it is "free" of specific allergens. This approach provides clear information, in a gentle and reassuring manner, for the end consumer.

GLUTEN-FREE

LACTOSE-FREE

MILK-FREE

Gluten-free desserts do not contain gluten, a protein found in wheat, barley, rye and their derivatives. Gluten-free desserts are essential for individuals with celiac disease or gluten intolerance and for those who choose to follow a gluten-free diet. These desserts often use alternative flours such as almond flour, coconut flour, rice flour, tapioca flour or gluten-free oat flour. **Be careful with beer: most traditional beers contain gluten because they are typically brewed from grains like barley, wheat and rye, all of which contain gluten.** It's important to ensure that gluten-free desserts are prepared in environments where cross-contamination with gluten-containing ingredients is avoided, using separate equipment and utensils.

Lactose-free desserts do not contain lactose, a sugar found in milk and dairy products. These desserts are suitable for individuals who are lactose intolerant, meaning they cannot properly digest lactose. Lactose-free desserts often use lactose-free milk, plant-based milks (such as almond, soy, coconut or oat milk), and dairy-free alternatives like margarine or coconut oil. It's important to ensure that lactose-free desserts are prepared in environments where cross-contamination with dairy products is avoided.

Milk-free in desserts means the dessert does not contain any milk or milk-derived ingredients. This is important for people who are lactose intolerant or who have a milk allergy. Milk-free desserts do not include milk, cream, butter, cheese, or any other dairy product ingredients. Instead, they use plant-based alternatives like almond milk, soy milk, coconut milk, oat milk, and dairy-free margarine.

NUT-FREE

SOY-FREE

VEGAN

Nut-free desserts do not contain any nuts or nut-derived ingredients. This is crucial for individuals with nut allergies, which can be severe and potentially life-threatening. These desserts exclude all types of nuts, such as almonds, walnuts, peanuts, cashews, hazelnuts, pistachios and other tree nuts. It's important to ensure that nut-free desserts are prepared in environments where cross-contamination with nuts is avoided, using separate equipment and utensils.

To claim a **soy-free** recipe, ensure all ingredients are free from soy and soy derivatives. Chocolate often contains soy lecithin for cost-effectiveness and to maintain viscosity during production. However, soy lecithin can slightly flatten the tasting notes of chocolate, making the complex flavors of high-quality cocoa less pronounced. All origins used in this book are soy lecithin-free to reveal the full taste of the cocoa.

Vegan desserts do not contain any animal-derived ingredients, making them suitable for individuals following a vegan diet, which excludes all animal products. Vegan desserts do not include ingredients like milk, eggs, butter, honey, gelatin or any other animal-derived products. Instead, they use plant-based alternatives such as almond milk, soy milk, coconut milk, flax eggs, chia seeds and vegan butter or margarine. Sweeteners like maple syrup, agave nectar, or coconut sugar are used instead of honey.

Please visit your local food safety authority's website for allergen regulations. There are more allergens than just the ones listed above.

To My Hands,

In my quiet moments of reflection, I'm amazed by the crucial role you play in my life and career. You are the quiet craftsmen, the unsung heroes of my chocolate journey, and today I want to thank you for your tireless dedication and unmatched skill.

From the first time I molded a piece of chocolate, you have been my loyal partners. With every gentle touch, you turn raw ingredients into beautiful works of art. The way you temper chocolate to a perfect shine, the precision with which you craft each praline, and the skill with which you pipe decorations—all this shows your exceptional talent and patience.

You have endured countless hours of work, braving the heat of the kitchen and the cold of the marble. Despite the challenges, you have stayed steady and accurate, turning my dreams into reality. Through you, I can share my passion and creativity with the world, and for that, I am eternally grateful.

You have mastered the balance between firmness and gentleness, ensuring each piece of chocolate and each dessert is both visually stunning and delicious. You understand the perfect pressure needed to create fine details and the delicate touch required for the most fragile confections and decorations.

In moments of doubt, you have given me the confidence to push limits and explore new techniques. You have been my constant companions, inspiring me to aim for excellence in every creation. Together we have built a legacy of art and craftsmanship, one piece of chocolate at a time.

So, to my hands, thank you for being the most valuable tools in my career. Your dedication and incredible skill have made all the difference. As we continue this journey together, I promise to care for you and always recognize your irreplaceable role in my life.

With deepest gratitude,
Michel Eyckerman

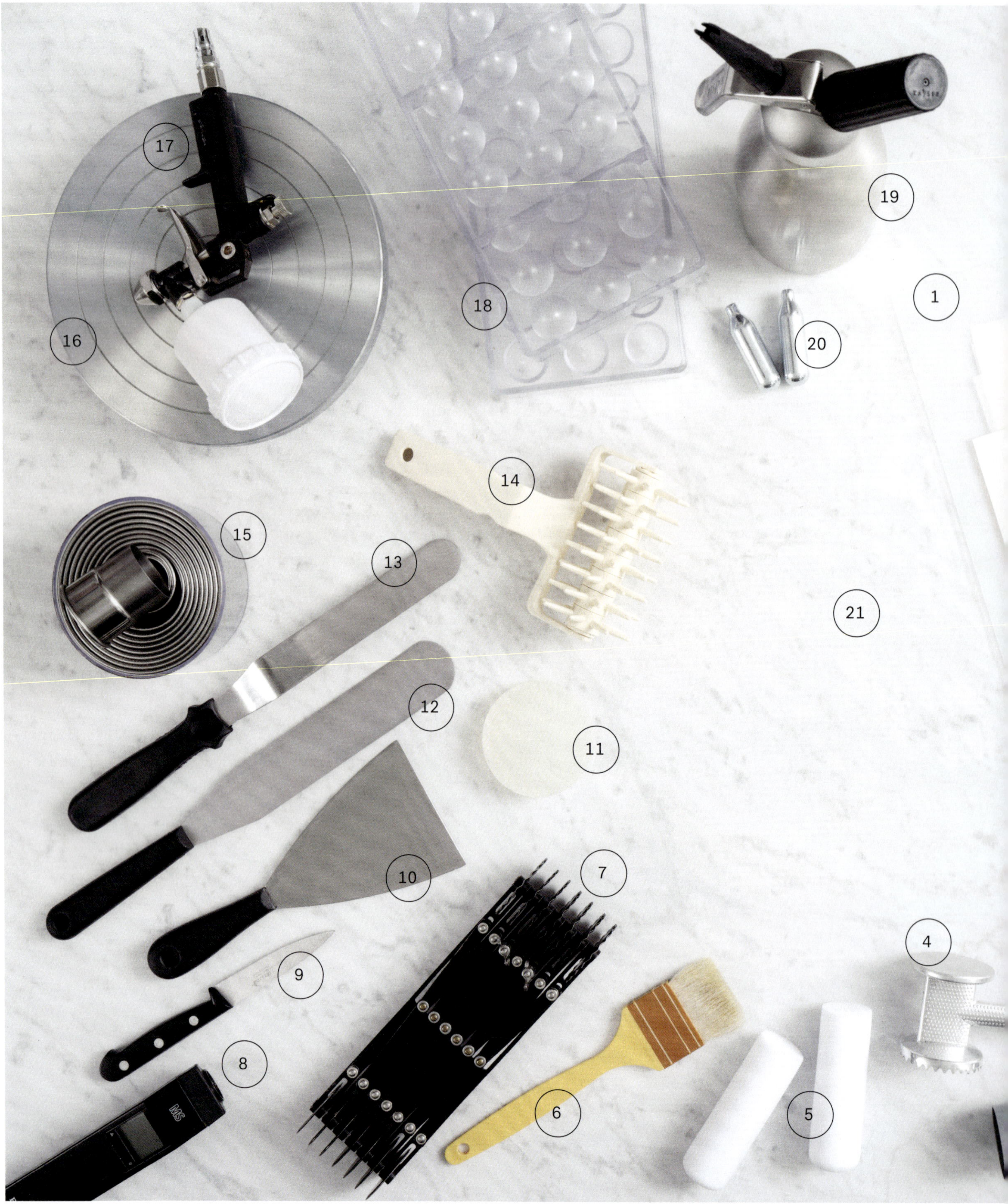
17
18
19
1
16
20
14
15
13
21
12
11
10
7
9
4
8
6
5

Tools

guitar sheets 1
baking paper 2
plastic tube 3
meat tenderizer 4
painting roller sponges 5
soft brush 6
bicycle cutter 7
laser thermometer 8
paring knife 9
triangle scraper 10
silicone stamp mold 11
spatula 12
offset spatula 13
plastic dough docker 14
dough cutters 15
ceramic spinning disc 16
spray gun 1mm needle 17
chocolate molds 18
siphon bottle 19
N_2O cartridges 20
granite table 21

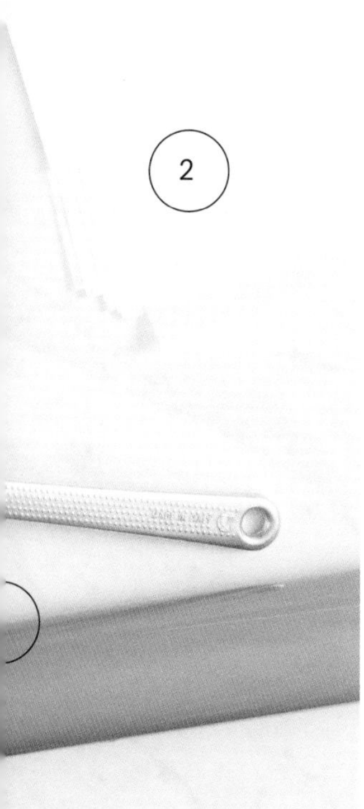

Guitar sheets: Also known as acetate sheets, typically made from polyethylene, this material is flexible, durable, and food-safe, making it ideal for chocolate decorations and pastry work.

Baking paper: Also known as parchment paper, it's used to line baking trays to prevent sticking and to make cleaning up easier. Suitable for making fragile chocolate decorations.

Plastic tube: Used for pushing the chocolate evenly between 2 guitar sheets. You can also roll chocolate decorations around it.

Meat tenderizer: A tool with a textured surface used to break down the fibers in meat, making it more tender. Here it's used to give a texture to chocolate decorations.

Painting roller sponges: Used for applying layers of colored cocoa butter on a guitar sheet.

Soft brush: Used for dusting some metallic powder on chocolate decorations or chocolate bonbons. Can be used to polish chocolate to obtain a more shiny finish.

Bicycle cutter: A multi-wheel cutter used to cut chocolate decorations into even strips or shapes.

Laser thermometer: A non-contact thermometer used to measure the surface temperature of ingredients like chocolate and colored cocoa butter. You can also take the temperature of the chocolate molds and other materials.

Paring knife: A small, versatile knife used for peeling, trimming and precise cutting tasks.

Triangle scraper: A tool with a triangular blade used for scraping and smoothing surfaces, often in chocolate work. Here I use it to temper chocolate.

Silicone stamp mold: Flexible molds used to create detailed shapes and structures of chocolate.

Spatula: A flat tool used for lifting, flipping and spreading food. To glaze the surface of mousse cakes.

Offset spatula: A spatula with a bend near the handle, for spreading out chocolate evenly on a surface. To pick up cake.

Plastic dough docker: A roller with spikes used to create small holes in dough, preventing it from puffing up excessively during baking. Here it's used to make small holes in chocolate decorations.

Dough cutters: Tool to cut sponge, dough or chocolate decorations into specific shapes or sizes.

Ceramic spinning disc: A rotating disc used for decorating cakes or pastries with precision. Can be used to make chocolate swirl decorations.

Spray gun 1mm needle: A spray tool with a 1mm needle used for applying fine layers of colored cocoa butter in molds or on chocolate decorations.

Chocolate molds: Polycarbonate molds used to shape chocolate into various forms and designs.

Siphon bottle: A pressurized bottle used for creating foams and mousses.

N_2O cartridges: Nitrous oxide cartridges used to charge siphon bottles for creating foams and mousses.

Granite table: Granite is a very hard and durable material, resistant to scratches and heat. This makes it ideal for repeated use in a kitchen environment. Granite naturally stays cool, which is crucial for tempering chocolate. The smooth, non-porous surface of granite makes it easy to spread and work with chocolate. It also helps in achieving a uniform thickness when rolling out chocolate or making decorations. Granite is non-porous when properly sealed, which means it doesn't harbor bacteria or absorb odors. This makes it a hygienic choice for food preparation, including chocolate work. You can also use a marble table, but it's more sensitive to scratches.

Tempering chocolate

The key ingredient in real chocolate that requires tempering is cocoa butter. **Cocoa butter** is a fat that can crystallize in several different forms, but only one of these forms (Form V) provides the properties desirable in high-quality chocolate.

Reasons for tempering

Formation of stable crystals
Tempering ensures the formation of stable cocoa butter crystals (Form V). These crystals give chocolate its smooth, glossy appearance and firm texture. Without tempering, the chocolate can form unstable crystals, leading to a dull finish and crumbly texture.

Preventing bloom
Bloom is a white, streaky appearance on the surface of chocolate; it is caused by unstable cocoa butter crystals. Bloomed chocolate looks unappealing and has a poor texture. Tempering prevents bloom by ensuring the formation of stable crystals.

Achieving the desired snap and texture
Properly tempered chocolate has a satisfying snap when breaking and a smooth mouthfeel. These qualities are indicators of high-quality chocolate and are achieved through the formation of stable cocoa butter crystals.

Shiny appearance
Tempered chocolate has a glossy, attractive finish, making it look more appealing. This shiny appearance is a sign of well-tempered chocolate and enhances its visual appeal.

Ease of mold release
Tempered chocolate contracts slightly as it cools down, making it easier to release from molds without sticking or breaking. This is crucial for creating molded chocolates and other confections.

Extending shelf life
Tempered chocolate has a longer shelf life and maintains its quality over time. It resists bloom and retains its texture, ensuring that the chocolate remains appealing and enjoyable.

The three key factors in tempering real chocolate

TEMPERATURE

Purpose
Temperature control is crucial in breaking down existing cocoa butter crystals and forming new, stable ones.

Process
- **Melting:** Heat chocolate to a specific temperature to break down all existing crystals.
- **Cooling:** Lower the temperature to encourage the formation of stable crystals (Form V).
- **Reheating:** Bring the chocolate to the working temperature while maintaining the stable crystals.

Importance
Precise temperature control ensures the chocolate has a smooth texture, shiny appearance and good snap.

MOVEMENT

Purpose
Continuous movement helps distribute the cocoa butter crystals evenly throughout the chocolate.

Process
- **Spreading and scraping:** Spread the chocolate thinly on a marble surface and continuously scrape and fold it to cool it down.
- **Stirring:** When using methods like seeding or microwaving, stir frequently to ensure even cooling and crystal formation.

Importance
Movement ensures that the stable crystals are evenly distributed, preventing bloom and ensuring a consistent texture.

TIME

Purpose
Time allows the cocoa butter crystals to form and stabilize properly.

Process
- **Cooling time:** Allow enough time for the chocolate to cool to the desired temperature.
- **Reheating time:** Ensure the chocolate is gently rewarmed to the working temperature without overheating.

Importance
Adequate time ensures that the stable crystals have formed correctly, resulting in well-tempered chocolate with a long shelf life and good structural integrity.

The actual tempering of real chocolate, starting from melting the chocolate

MELTING

Process
Put the chocolate in a plastic bowl and melt it gently in a microwave at medium power, stirring frequently to ensure even melting; or melt the chocolate in a dry heater or heating chamber.
- **Dark Chocolate:** Heat to 45-50 °C
- **Milk Chocolate:** Heat to 45 °C
- **White Chocolate:** Heat to 43-45 °C

COOLING

Process
Pour 4/5 of the melted chocolate onto the marble surface. Use a chocolate scraper or spatula to spread the chocolate thinly across the marble. Continuously scrape and fold the chocolate to cool it to the desired temperature. This process encourages the formation of stable cocoa butter crystals (Form V).
- **Dark Chocolate:** Cool to 28 °C
- **Milk Chocolate:** Cool to 27 °C
- **White Chocolate:** Cool to 26.5 °C

REHEATING

Process
Scrape the cooled chocolate back into the bowl with the remaining warm chocolate. Mix thoroughly to ensure an even temperature as you heat the chocolate back up to the working temperature while maintaining the stable crystals.
- **Dark Chocolate:** Reheat to 30 °C
- **Milk Chocolate:** Reheat to 29 °C
- **White Chocolate:** Reheat to 28 °C

TIPS FOR ALL TYPES

Keep tools dry
Ensure all tools and surfaces are completely clean and dry to prevent the chocolate from seizing.

Maintain Temperature
Keep the tempered chocolate at the working temperature while using it. If it cools down too much, gently reheat it with a heating gun.

Average working temperature of tempered chocolate
The working temperatures above are general. For each type of chocolate, the tempering can be slightly different. For example, for a dark chocolate with a higher cocoa butter content, you'll need to lower the working temperature of the tempered chocolate. A dark chocolate of 73% is to be used at approximately 29.4 °C instead of 31 °C for a 55% dark chocolate.

Tests to see if the chocolate is well-tempered or pre-crystalized

Cooling test
Dip a knife or a piece of parchment paper into the chocolate, then chill it at room temperature (20 °C) for 2 minutes. Now transfer it into a cool fridge for 3 minutes. If the chocolate sets with a glossy finish and a clean snap, it's well-tempered.

Visual inspection
Properly tempered chocolate should have a shiny, glossy finish. If it looks dull or streaky, it might not be well-tempered.
Texture test: Properly tempered chocolate should feel smooth and firm at room temperature (20 °C). It should not be sticky or soft.

Texture test
Properly tempered chocolate should feel smooth and firm at room temperature (20 °C). It should not be sticky or soft.

Snap test
Break a piece of chocolate. Well-tempered chocolate will break cleanly with a sharp snap. If it bends or crumbles, it's not properly tempered.

Different methods of tempering chocolate

There are several methods for tempering chocolate, each with its own advantages. Here are the main ones:

TABLING METHOD

Process
Melt chocolate, pour 4/5 onto a marble surface, cool by spreading and scraping, then combine with reserved warm chocolate following the tempering curve of heating, cooling and reheating.

Advantages
Provides excellent control over the tempering process and is ideal for large quantities. Good for all chocolate work, decorations, molding, dipping and enrobing.

SEEDING METHOD

Process
Melt chocolate to the required temperature, add finely tempered chocolate drops (seeds) to cool and stabilize, stir until fully melted and tempered.

Advantages
Easier and less messy than tabling, suitable for smaller batches.

SOUS-VIDE METHOD

Process
Place chocolate in a vacuum-sealed bag, melt in a sous vide water bath at precise temperatures, agitate to ensure even tempering.

Advantages
Precise temperature control, minimal mess, ideal for consistent results. Good for making chocolate decorations.

MAGIC TEMPER METHOD

Process
Heat the chocolate to around 45 °C. Add 1% cocoa butter silk when the chocolate is at 33.5-34 °C, then cool to the working temperature (31-32 °C for dark chocolate, 29-30 °C for milk chocolate, 28-29 °C for white chocolate).

Advantages
Quick and convenient, suitable for small quantities.

DIRECT METHOD

Process
Melt chocolate directly in a tempering machine, which maintains the correct temperature and agitation.

Advantages
Automated process, ideal for commercial use.

Each method has its advantages; the choice depends on the quantity of chocolate, available equipment and personal preference.

The basics of making molded and colored pralines

First, some general conditions when working with chocolate

- Clean the molds with cotton and some pure alcohol.
- Keep the relative humidity in the working area and fridge below 60% at all times.
- The ideal temperature in the working area is 20 °C.
- Always use well-tempered chocolate.
- Leave the chocolate to set in the mold on the work surface before putting it in the fridge.
- Leave molds filled with chocolate to crystallize on a wire rack to allow aircirculation completely around the mold.
- Use polycarbonate molds; they are the easiest to work with and they give aperfect finished aspect.
- To color the molds with colored cocoa butter, use fat-soluble colors in powder, natural colors in powder or fruit powders.

Methods of coloring

INGREDIENTS

Colored cocoa butter

Pure Prime Pressed Cocoa Butter	100 g
fat-soluble coloring powder	10 g

Chocolate spray

Selection White, Milk or Dark chocolat	100 g
Pure Prime Pressed Cocoa Butter	120 g

Metallic cocoa butter spray coloring

Pure Prime Pressed Cocoa Butter	100 g
metallic coloring powder	8 g

Metallic pure alcohol spray coloring

metallic coloring powder	6 g
pure alcohol (food grade ethanol)	100 g

Two innovative tips

METHOD

Colored cocoa butter
Heat the cocoa butter to 45 °C and add the coloring powder.
Mix with an immersion blender.
Pour into small plastic cups and close with a lid.
Keep warm in a heating chamber at 40 °C or leave to cool down and reheat later.

- Yellow = 9 g yellow coloring powder per 100 g cocoa butter.
- Green = 8 g yellow and 1 g blue coloring powder per 100 g cocoa butter.
- Dark green = 6 g yellow and 3 g blue coloring powder per 100 g cocoa butter.
- Orange = 7 g yellow and 2 g red coloring powder per 100 g cocoa butter.
- Red = 8 g red and 1 g yellow coloring powder per 100 g cocoa butter.
- Blue = 9 g blue coloring powder per 100 g cocoa butter.
- Purple = 6 g blue coloring powder and 3 g red coloring powder per 100 g cocoa butter.
- Black = 3 g blue, 3 g red and 3 g yellow coloring powder per 100 g cocoa butter.

Chocolate spray
Heat both ingredients to 40 °C.
Temper to 30 °C on a marble table.
Spray in chocolate polycarbonate molds of 20 °C.
Leave to crystallize for 30 minutes before molding.

Metallic cocoa butter spray coloring
Heat the cocoa butter to 45 °C and add the metallic coloring powder.
Use bronze, silver or gold metallic powder.
Mix with an immersion blender.
Pour into small plastic cups and close with a lid.
Keep warm in a heating chamber at 40 °C or leave to cool down and reheat later.

Metallic pure alcohol spray coloring
Use bronze, silver or gold metallic powder.
Mix the metallic coloring powder with the pure alcohol.
Pour into small plastic cups and close with a lid.
You can use this to give a sparkling touch to your molded chocolate bonbons.
Spray this color with alcohol into your chocolate molds.
The pure alcohol will evaporate, leaving only the metallic coloring powder in the chocolate molds.

First, some preparations for easy and correct tempering of colored cocoa butter

- Put the bowl of a robot cutter and the blade in the fridge for about 10 minutes. See picture on page 48.
- Put 200 g of cocoa butter drops in the bowl and cut the cocoa butter into small pieces of 1 mm.
- For an even result, you can pass the cut cocoa butter through a sieve of 2mm.
- Keep this powder stored in a closed container at room temperature (20 °C).

The M50 rule

- For coloring with cocoa butter, the ideal temperature of the mold is 20 °C.
  Your colored cocoa butter should be tempered at 30 °C.
- According to the M50 rule, you have a few degrees of flexibility.
- When the mold is a bit cooler (18 °C), you should apply tempered colored cocoa butter at 32 °C. Together this adds up to 50.
- When your mold is a bit warmer (22 °C), you should apply tempered colored cocoa butter a bit cooler (28 °C). Together, this adds up to 50.
- The ideal temperature of the mold is 20 °C, with a minimum of 18 °C and a maximum 22 °C. You have 4 °C to play with, which is a lot in chocolate-making.

See the table below.

Mold Temperature	Min 18 °C	Best 20 °C	Max 22 °C
Colored Cocoa butter	32 °C	30 °C	28 °C

The M50 rule: 20 + 30 = 50
18 + 32 = 50
22 + 28 = 50

The M from the M50 rule comes from MICHEL. ☺

Spraying molds with tempered colored cocoa butter

How to spray your polycarbonate molds with cocoa butter perfectly every time

- Take the temperature of the mold with a laser thermometer. The best temperature is 20 °C.

- Put 100 g of colored cocoa butter in a small plastic cup that you can close with a lid.
- Heat the colored cocoa butter to 40 °C.
- When it reaches 38 °C, add 2% of the cocoa butter powder, that you made before (see p. 49) (2 g or 1 teaspoon).

- Close the plastic cup with the lid and shake for about 15 seconds.
- Put it on the table and wait until the cocoa butter reaches 30 °C (see picture; mold is 20 °C, M50 rule).

- Transfer the tempered colored cocoa butter to the spray gun and start spraying, decorating your molds as desired.

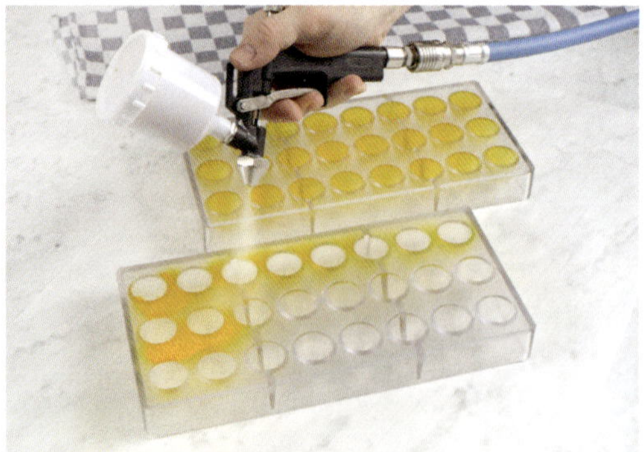

- When the molds are colored, clean the top surface of the mold with a scraper to recover excess colored cocoa butter.
- For larger productions, reheat your spray gun occasionally with a heating gun to keep it at the correct temperature.
- Leave the colored molds to set for 30 minutes at room temperature (20 °C) before molding chocolate.

Molding and filling

- Use a piping bag to fill the molds with tempered chocolate.
- Tap the filled mold against the table to remove any air bubbles.
- Flip the mold above a sheet of baking paper to recover the excess chocolate.
- Next, tap against the mold with a spatula to make a thin layer of chocolate on the inside of the polycarbonate mold.
- Leave the filled molds to set for 5 minutes at room temperature (20 °C). (I put them on the table sideways.)

- Clean the surface of the molds with a metal scraper and put the molds on a 40 x 60 cm pastry grill.
- Put the molds in a fridge for chocolate at a temperature of 16 °C and a humidity level below 60%.
- Leave the molds to crystallize for one hour before filling them.
- Fill the molds with a prepared filling; the required temperature of the filling will depend on the chocolate you used for molding.

Chocolate shell	White	Milk	Dark
T° filling	28 °C	29 °C	30 °C

- Leave the filling to crystallize before closing with tempered chocolate. In general, when you fill a chocolate shell with a ganache you should leave it to crystallize overnight.

Closing and demolding

- Heat the surface of the filled mold a bit with a heating gun and pipe some tempered chocolate into the filled cavities.
- You can scrape the excess chocolate away with a metal scraper or spatula, or you can put a transfer sheet on top (see picture) and clean the top of the mold by pushing off the excess chocolate with a metal scraper.

- Put the closed mold in the fridge for about 5 minutes and unmold.
- If you closed the mold with a transfer sheet, wait 30 minutes before you remove the transfer sheet and do the unmolding.
- To avoid sugar bloom, store the finished chocolates or bonbons in a cool dry place at 16 °C, always with an average humidity level below 60%.

Decoration
The first step

MATERIALS

The first step

Selection Dark 55% chocolate	as needed
guitar sheet	2
baking paper	1
plastic tube	1

METHOD

The first step

- Always work on a granite or a marble surface, especially when you are tempering chocolate or making chocolate decorations.
- Put a piece of baking paper on the marble surface to better see the working surface where you will pour your tempered chocolate.
- Place a plastic guitar sheet on top of the baking paper and position it vertically in front of you on the surface.
- Pour a strip of approximately 150 g of tempered chocolate onto the guitar sheet and place a second guitar sheet on top.
- Use a plastic tube to push the chocolate from your side to the other end of the guitar sheets.
- The objective is to push the chocolate in one smooth movement from one side to the other, achieving the correct thickness between the two guitar sheets.
- You can repeat this movement a couple of times to ensure the chocolate is evenly spread between the two guitar sheets.
- Leave the chocolate to crystallize for at least an hour in a cool and dry place, or immediately proceed with the next step to create other textures or shapes.
- There is no need to put a tray on the chocolate decoration, as the chocolate has been spread out between two guitar sheets.
- Unmold the chocolate decoration from the guitar sheets just before use.
- You can also do this technique with other types of chocolate, like milk, white or amber chocolate.

Decoration Token

MATERIALS

Token

Selection Dark 55% chocolate	as needed
guitar sheet	2
plastic tube	1
dough cutters	1

METHOD

Token

- Using a plastic tube, spread tempered chocolate between two guitar sheets (see p. 52).
- To ensure a clean cut of the chocolate decoration, wait for the correct moment to press the dough cutters into the guitar sheet.
- Leave to crystallize for at least an hour in a cool and dry place.
- Unmold the chocolate decoration from the guitar sheets.

Decoration
Perforation

MATERIALS

Perforation

Selection Dark 55% chocolate	as needed
guitar sheet	2
plastic tube	1
fluted dough cutter 6 cm	1
plastic dough docker	1

METHOD

Perforation

- Spread out tempered chocolate between two guitar sheets by using a plastic tube (see p. 52).
- Immediately start rolling the plastic dough docker over the guitar sheet to create small indentations in the chocolate.
- To ensure a clean cut of the chocolate decoration, wait for the correct moment to push the fluted dough cutters into the guitar sheet.
- Leave to crystallize for at least an hour in a cool and dry place.
- Unmold the chocolate decoration from the guitar sheets.

Decoration Pixel

MATERIALS

Pixel

Selection Milk 35% chocolate	as needed
guitar sheet	2
silicone sheet	1
plastic tube	1
dough cutter 6 cm	1
meat tenderizer	1

METHOD

Pixel

- Spread tempered chocolate between two guitar sheets with a plastic tube (see p. 52).
- Immediately move the guitar sheets with the chocolate in between to a silicone baking sheet.
- Wait for the correct moment to press down on the top guitar sheet with the meat tenderizer to transfer the texture into the chocolate.
- Push the meat tenderizer into the guitar sheet with both hands.
- Cut out rounds a bit larger than the structure created in the chocolate.
- Leave to crystallize for at least an hour in a cool and dry place.
- Unmold the chocolate decoration from the guitar sheets.

Decoration Mosaic

MATERIALS

Mosaic

Selection Dark 55% chocolate	as needed
yellow colored cocoa butter	10 g
blue colored cocoa butter	10 g
flat plastic container	1
silver powder	2 g
soft brush	1
painting roller sponges	1
guitar sheet	2
plastic tube	1
bicycle cutter (the fluted side)	1

METHOD

Mosaic

- Temper the yellow and blue cocoa butter to 30 °C and place them in a flat plastic container, with the yellow on one side and the blue on the other.
- Put a guitar sheet on the marble surface.
- Dip the painting roller sponge into the yellow and blue cocoa butter and paint the guitar sheet, moving from left to right.
- Do this movement with the paint roller sponge until the guitar sheet is colored enough.
- Stop moving the paint roller sponge when the colored cocoa butter feels dry.
- Next, brush the colored cocoa butter with some silver powder using a soft brush.
- Put the colored guitar sheet aside and place a new guitar sheet on the work surface.
- Pour a line of approximately 150 g of tempered dark chocolate on the new guitar sheet and put the colored guitar sheet on top of it.
- Push the dark chocolate in one smooth movement from one side to the other using the plastic tube.
- Leave to set for 30 seconds and cut squares of the desired size with the bicycle cutter.
- Leave to crystallize for at least one hour in a cool and dry place.
- Unmold the chocolate decoration from the guitar sheet.

Decoration Woody

MATERIALS

Woody

Selection Dark 55% chocolate	as needed
Selection Amber 30% chocolate	as needed
guitar sheet	2
plastic tube	1
dough cutters	1

METHOD

Woody

- Pour a line of approximately 50 g of tempered dark chocolate directly onto the marble surface.
- Immediately place a guitar sheet on top of the chocolate and push the chocolate away to the other side of the guitar sheet with a plastic tube.
- Pull off the guitar sheet straightaway to create a woody design.
- Leave to set for 1 minute.
- Take a second guitar sheet and place it on the surface.
- Pour a line of approximately 150 g of tempered amber chocolate on the second guitar sheet.
- Put the guitar sheet with the woody design on top and push the tempered amber chocolate between the two guitar sheets from one side to the other using a plastic tube.
- To ensure a clean cut of the chocolate decoration, wait for the correct moment to push the dough cutters into the guitar sheet.
- Leave to crystallize for at least an hour in a cool and dry place.
- Unmold the chocolate decoration from the guitar sheets.

Decoration Sunny

MATERIALS

Sunny

Selection White Intense 31% chocolate	as needed
yellow colored cocoa butter	40 g
fat-soluble red coloring powder	1 g
spray gun with 1 mm needle	1
guitar sheet	2
baking paper	1
plastic tube	1
dough cutters, 6 cm diameter	1

METHOD

Sunny

- Draw lines on a baking sheet to mark where you will spray the colored cocoa butter.
- Put a guitar sheet on top of the baking sheet.
- Temper the yellow cocoa butter to 30 °C and put it in the spray gun.
- Put a little bit of red color powder in the spray gun on top of the yellow cocoa butter that you have already added.
- Close the spray gun and shake a bit.
- Spray a dot of colored cocoa butter on the guitar sheet, but stay at the same place; don't move the spray gun while you spray.
- Now release pressure on the handle of the spray gun until only air is coming out.
- Use the jet of air to spread out the spot of yellow you have sprayed until you achieve the result shown in the picture.
- Repeat this technique until you have made enough decorations and leave to crystallize for 15 minutes.
- Now pour approximately 150 g of tempered white chocolate onto another guitar sheet and place the guitar sheet with the yellow sprayed circles on top.
- Push the chocolate in one smooth movement from one side to the other using the plastic tube (see p. 52)
- Place the dough cutters in the correct position and press into the guitar sheet to cut the chocolate.
- Leave to crystallize for at least an hour in a cool and dry place.
- Unmold the chocolate decoration from the guitar sheet.

Decoration Structured

MATERIALS

Structured

Selection Dark 55% chocolate	as needed
Selection Milk 35% chocolate	as needed
Selection White Intense 31% chocolate	as needed
structured sheet	2
offset spatula	1
dough cutters	1
baking paper	1
heavy tray	1

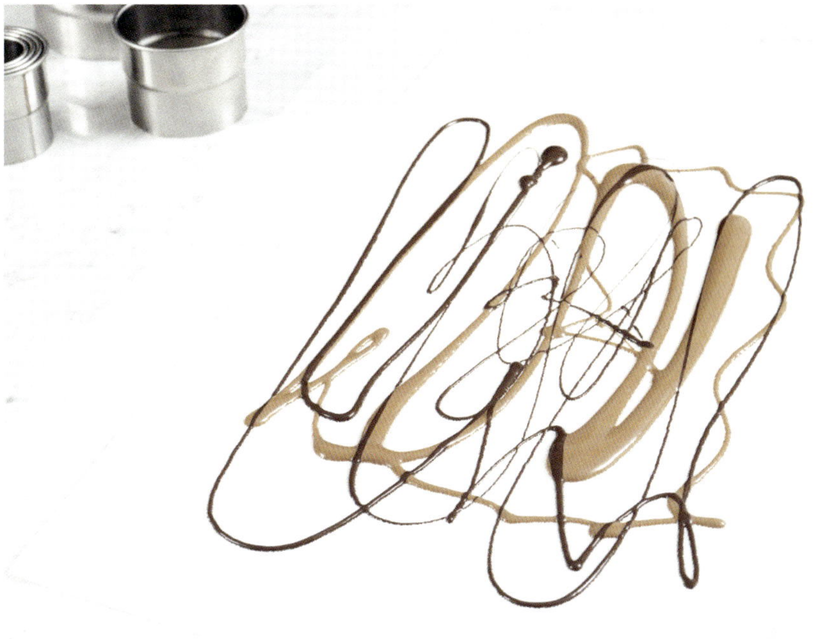

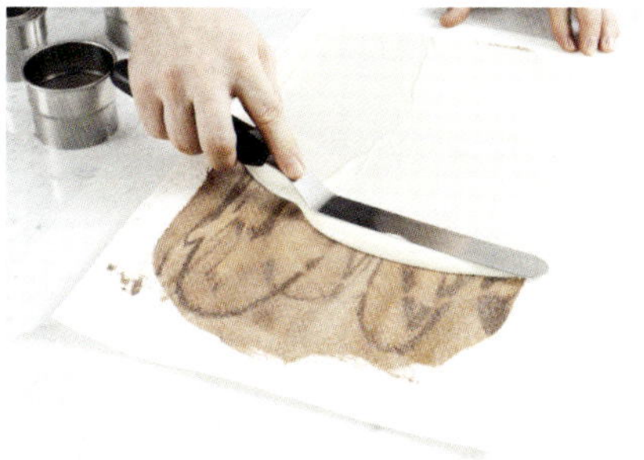

METHOD

Structured

- Take a food-safe structured sheet.
- Put a little bit of tempered dark and milk chocolate on the structured sheet and spread it out very thin with an offset spatula.
- Cover the whole with a layer of tempered white chocolate.
- Leave to crystallize for a minute until dry to the touch.
- Cut out rounds with dough cutters and put a sheet of baking paper on top.
- To prevent bending of the decoration, put a heavy tray on top.
- Leave to crystallize for at least an hour in a cool and dry place.
- Unmold the chocolate decoration from the structured sheet.

Decoration Yellow rings

MATERIALS

Yellow rings

Selection White Intense	
31% chocolate	100 g
yellow-colored cocoa butter	10 g
mandolin cutter knife 1 cm	1
inox circles, 7 cm diameter	1
metal ruler	1
offset spatula	1
rhodoïde strips	as needed
tape	as needed

METHOD

Yellow rings

- Mix the yellow-colored cocoa butter with the white chocolate and temper it to 28 °C on a marble surface.
- Take a rhodoïde strip and put it on the table.
- Spread a thin layer of tempered yellow chocolate over it using an offset spatula.
- Leave the chocolate on the rhodoïde strip to crystallize for 1 minute.
- Place the Rhodoïde strip against a metal ruler and use the ruler as a guide to cut the chocolate with a mandoline knife.
- Once cut, place the rhodoïde immediately around a stainless steel ring and tape it so it stays in position.
- You can repeat this procedure as needed.
- Leave to crystallize for at least an hour in a cool and dry place.
- Gently unmold the chocolate decoration from the rhodoïde strip.

Decoration Cococoins

MATERIALS

Cococoins

Selection White Intense 31% chocolate	as needed
baking paper	2
stencil 4 cm diameter	1
grated coconut	1

METHOD

Cococoins

- Take the stencil and put it on a sheet of baking paper.
- Put the dosage container on the stencil and pour some tempered white chocolate into it.
- Slide the dosage container from one side to the other.
- Remove the stencil immediately and sprinkle some grated coconut over the chocolate.
- You can repeat this procedure as needed.
- Leave to crystallize for at least an hour in a cool and dry place.
- Unmold the chocolate decoration from the baking paper.
- You can also make this chocolate decoration with other types of chocolate and sprinkle other ingredients over it.

Decoration Spikes

MATERIALS

Spikes

Selection Dark 55% chocolate	as needed
marble or granite surface	1
offset spatula	1
chef's knife	1

METHOD

Spikes

- Spread out a strip of tempered dark chocolate approximately 20 cm wide and 1 mm thick on the marble surface.
- Leave the chocolate to crystallize for a minute.
- Wait for the correct moment to make the chocolate decoration.
- Hold the chef's knife at a 45-degree angle and smoothly pull it towards yourself through the chocolate to create long, elegant spikes.
- Leave them to crystallize for at least 30 minutes in a cool and dry place.

Decoration Swirl

MATERIALS

Swirl

Selection Dark 55% chocolate	as needed
ceramic spinning disc	1
baking paper	1
baking spray or some oil	1
spoon	1

METHOD

Swirl

- Cut a sheet of baking paper into 15 cm squares.
- Spray some baking spray on top of the ceramic spinning disc and put a square of baking paper on top.
- Pipe about 8 g of tempered chocolate in the middle of the square.
- Immediately give the spinner a manual spin at high speed.
- While the disc is spinning, press down gently on the chocolate with a spoon, moving from the center towards the side of the spinner.
- Stop when you have reached a good size for the swirl decoration.
- Remove the decoration from the disc by taking the baking paper by two corners and moving it to a tray.
- Leave to crystallize for at least an hour in a cool and dry place.
- Unmold the chocolate decoration from the baking paper.

Decoration Vortex

MATERIALS

Vortex

Selection White Intense 31% chocolate	as needed
silicone stamp mold	1
cool spray	1

METHOD

Vortex

- Put the silicone stamp in the freezer.
- Draw lines on a sheet of baking paper to mark where to pipe the chocolate.
- Pipe drops of tempered white chocolate approximately 8 g each onto the baking paper.
- Place the frozen silicone stamp on top of each chocolate drop and immediately press it down gently with one finger in the middle of the silicone stamp.
- Remove the stamp and make the next vortex decoration.
- Between each one, spray some cool spray on the silicone stamp to keep it frozen each time you make another chocolate vortex decoration.
- Leave to crystallize for at least an hour in a cool and dry place.
- Unmold the chocolate decoration from the baking paper.

Decoration Aero

MATERIALS

Aero

Selection Milk 35%	250 g
Pure Prime Pressed Cocoa Butter	25 g
grapeseed (or other) oil	10 g
guitar sheet	1
baking paper	1
siphon bottle	1
N_2O cartridges	2
plexi or transparent plate	1

METHOD

Aero

- Heat the Selection Milk 35% chocolate and the Pure Prime Pressed Cocoa Butter to 45 °C and temper it to 32 °C on a marble surface.
- Add the grapeseed oil and mix with a spatula.
- Transfer this composition into a Siphon® bottle and close it.
- Charge the Siphon® bottle with two N_2O cartridges and shake well after each.
- Pipe small dots onto a strip of a guitar sheet and press down with another sheet until the dots are 1 mm thick.
- Allow to crystallize for at least an hour in a cool and dry place.
- Unmold the chocolate decoration from the guitar sheets.

Chocolate sourdough thyme waffle

Transferring the flavor of a ligneous plant into chocolate via frying in cocoa butter is a beautiful technique. This flavored cocoa butter is then used to make the chocolate waffle. The sourdough rye bread crumbs give a crunchy touch.

COMPONENTS

For 70 pieces of 9 g
Thyme cocoa butter
Rye bread crumbs

CHOCOLATE AND BEER PAIRING

The fruity, floral notes and subtle spice of Deus Brut Des Flandres complement the thyme-infused Peru 64% dark chocolate waffle. The rye sourdough bread crumbs add depth, creating a complex but balanced flavor combination.

INGREDIENTS

Thyme cocoa butter

fresh thyme	30 g
Pure Prime Pressed Cocoa Butter	100 g

Rye bread crumbs
2 g/portion

rye sourdough bread	300 g

Chocolate waffle
7 g/portion

Peru 64% dark chocolate	400 g
thyme cocoa butter	80 g

PREPARATION

Thyme cocoa butter
Wash the fresh thyme with water.
Heat the cocoa butter to 150 °C.
Fry the fresh thyme in the heated cocoa butter for about 3 minutes until all the moisture cooks out of the thyme.
Leave it to cool and set aside overnight.
Reheat the infused cocoa butter and strain to remove the thyme.
Use this flavored cocoa butter in the recipe "chocolate waffle".

Rye bread crumbs
Buy a fresh-baked, quality Sourdough rye bread with a good acidity from a bakery.
Cut the bread into thin slices of 3 to 5 mm thickness.
Put the slices on a baking tray and dry bake at 140 °C with damper open (or prop open the oven door with a spoon while baking) for about 30 minutes.
Crush the slices of dry sourdough rye bread to obtain small crumbs.
The best method is to push the bread through a sieve with a mesh size of 2 mm.

Chocolate waffle
Combine the Peru 64% dark chocolate and the thyme cocoa butter and heat to 45 °C.
Temper the chocolate on a marble table to 29 °C.
Pour into polycarbonate waffle molds and shake to remove any air bubbles.
Immediately sprinkle the top with the sourdough rye bread crumbs.
Leave to crystallize for 1 hour in a cool place (approximately 15 °C) with a relative humidity level below 60%.
Unmold and pack them in a closed plastic container sealed with a lid to keep the bread crumbs crunchy.
Mold: Chocolate World CW1626

Chocolate spread upcycled beer bread

Spread our beer chocolate spread on beer-flavored bread for a decadent twist on a classic snack. This delightful recipe combines the rich taste of chocolate with the bold flavor of a strong beer for a unique treat.

COMPONENTS

For one 900 g bread
10 pots
of 120 g chocolate spread
Beer bread with beer draff
Beer chocolate spread

CHOCOLATE AND BEER PAIRING

Rich, fruity notes and mild caramel bitterness in St Bernardus Abt 12 pair beautifully with the acidic, citrusy Vietnam 73% dark chocolate beer spread, creating a balanced flavor experience.

INGREDIENTS

Beer bread with beer draff

St Bernardus Abt 12 beer	100 g
beer draff	200 g
water	150 g
strong bread flour	450 g
fresh yeast	10 g
olive oil	20 g
salt	6 g

Beer chocolate spread

sugar	130 g
glucose	115 g
Isomalt	110 g
cream (35% fat)	220 g
St Bernardus Abt 12 beer	180 g
invert sugar	45 g
dry butter 99% or ghee	120 g
almond praliné 50%	75 g
Vietnam 73% dark chocolate	240 g
Vietnam 45% milk chocolate	50 g

PREPARATION

Beer bread with beer draff

Pour the beer over the beer draff and let it soak for 15 minutes.
Blend this mixture with an immersion blender to make the barley from the beer draff less sharp.
In a mixer with the kneading attachment, knead all ingredients except for the salt and the olive oil for 2 minutes at medium speed.
Add the salt and the olive oil and knead for 3 minutes at medium speed and 6 minutes at medium-high speed (adjust the dough texture by adding some extra flour if needed).
Dough temperature should be 26 °C.
Cover the bowl of the mixer with cling film and let the dough rest for 10 minutes.
Give a first proof of 15 minutes.
Flatten the dough a bit with your hands and shape the dough into an oval.
Dust some flour on the shaped bread and give a second proof of about 1 hour.
After proofing, the dough should have doubled in size.
Bake at 230 °C with some steam at the beginning and closed dampers for about 30 minutes.
Lower the temperature to 210 °C and bake another 10 minutes with open dampers.
Take the bread out of the oven and let it cool down on a wire rack.

TIP ⟶ *If you don't have beer draff, you can also use crushed wheat flour or whole wheat flour.*

Beer chocolate spread

Make a blond caramel with the sugar, glucose and isomalt.
Heat the cream and the beer to 80 °C.
Deglaze the caramel with it and pour this warm component over all other ingredients.
Mix with a spatula until smooth, then mix with an immersion blender.
Try to avoid incorporating air bubbles while mixing.
When the beer chocolate spread is finished, transfer to glass jars (allow to cool before sealing the jars).
Refrigerate after sealing.
Shelf life: 1 month in a closed jar when stored in a cool, dry place.

TIP ⟶ *If you don't have isomalt, you can use sugar, but the flavor will be a bit sweeter.*

Chocolate grissini

Indulge in the perfect blend of savory and sweet with these rosemary grissini, elegantly coated in rich Uganda 80% dark chocolate and adorned with a sprinkle of tangy blue salt.

BREAD 'N SPREAD

COMPONENTS

For 50 grissini of 25 g
Rosemary grissini
Coating & finishing

CHOCOLATE AND BEER PAIRING

Grandgousier de la Lienne's refreshing, hoppy notes and subtle bitterness complement the intense, roasted cocoa of Uganda 80% dark chocolate. Sea salt and rosemary add a savory, aromatic finish to the grissini.

INGREDIENTS

Rosemary grissini
15 g/grissini

bread flour	400 g
semolina flour	100 g
water	270 g
fresh yeast	10 g
dried rosemary	6 g
olive oil	40 g
salt	10 g

Coating & finishing
10 g/grissini

Uganda 80% dark chocolate	500 g
Persian blue salt	as needed
dried rosemary	as needed

PREPARATION

Rosemary grissini

In a mixer with the kneading attachment, knead all ingredients except the salt and olive oil for 1 minute at medium speed.
Add the salt and knead for 4 minutes at medium speed and 7 minutes at high speed.
Add the olive oil and knead another minute at medium speed.
Dough temperature should be 26 °C.
Cover the dough with cling film and let rest on a work surface for 10 minutes.
Sprinkle with some semolina flour and flatten the dough out to 3 mm.
Let rise for about an hour.
Using a sharp knife, slice the dough into narrow strands.
Put them on a baking tray and leave to rise for another 30 minutes.
Bake at 220 °C with closed dampers for about 10 minutes and then lower the temperature to 200 °C.
Bake for another 10 minutes with open dampers until dry.
Set the grissini aside to cool.

Coating and finishing

Heat the Uganda 80% dark chocolate to approximately 48 °C and temper on a marble slab to 29,4 °C.
Enrobe the middle of the grissini with the tempered dark chocolate and decorate immediately with some blue salt and dried rosemary.
Leave to crystallize at room temperature (about 20 °C) for 30 minutes.
Store in a cool, dry place with a relative humidity level below 60%. Store them in a closed container.

Predinner Pleasures

Chia parmesan chocolate thins

The umami of Parmesan combines with the chia seeds' crunch and white chocolate's creamy sweetness to create an exciting blend of textures and flavors. Together, they deliver a surprising yet delightful culinary experience.

COMPONENTS

For 25 pieces of 15 g
Parmesan chia thins

CHOCOLATE AND BEER PAIRING

Orval beer's fruity, slightly acidic profile complements the sweet, creamy white chocolate. The nutty, umami-rich Parmesan cheese balances the beer's bitterness, while chia seeds add a mild, nutty flavor and crunchy texture, creating a harmony.

INGREDIENTS

Parmesan chia thins
15 g/portion

parmesan cheese	75 g
chia seeds	25 g
Selection White Intense 31% chocolate	250 g
Pure Prime Pressed Cocoa Butter	25 g
sea salt	0.5 g

PREPARATION

Parmesan chia thins
Grate the parmesan cheese with a rasp.
Bake the grated parmesan cheese in the oven at 150 °C until dry and golden brown.
Set aside to cool and then pulse in a blender into a fine crumble.
Roast the chia seeds in a pan and set them aside to cool down.
Combine the Selection White Intense 31% chocolate and cocoa butter and heat to 45 °C.
Temper to 29 °C on a marble slab.
Add the parmesan crumble, the roasted chia seeds and the sea salt and mix gently with a spatula.
Spread this composition out on a sheet of baking paper to a thickness of 2 mm.
Leave to set a bit until just dry and cut immediately into long triangles.
Put them on a corrugated sheet and leave to crystallize.
Store in a closed container in a cool place (around 16 °C).

Salty chocolate ribbed chips

Eating chips and drinking a refreshing beer during a barbecue or a football game is a Belgian tradition. Only one thing was missing, the chocolate—until now! This easy-to-make salty chocolate snack is a must-have for a gathering with friends.

COMPONENTS

For approximately 20 servings
Spray chocolate
Salty ribbed chips

CHOCOLATE AND BEER PAIRING

Bavik Super Pils' crisp, clean taste complements the salty crunch of potato chips. The robust, earthy flavors of Uganda 80% dark chocolate add depth and creates a balance.

INGREDIENTS

Spray chocolate
1 g ratio

Uganda 80% dark chocolate	100 g
Pure Prime Pressed Cocoa Butter	15 g

Salty ribbed chips
5 g ratio

salty ribbed potato chips	250 g

PREPARATION

Spray chocolate
Combine the Uganda 80% dark chocolate and cocoa butter and heat to 50 °C.
Temper to 30 °C on a marble slab.
Keep this tempered chocolate at 30 °C to apply it with a brush on the salted potato chips.

Salty Ribbed Chips
Buy good-quality salted ribbed potato chips.
Make sure you only use the best ones, leaving out any broken or crumbled chips in the bag.
For this creation I put the chips in a metal rotating drum and then spray the tempered chocolate composition on the chips.
You can also use a soft brush to apply the tempered chocolate to cover the salty ribbed potato chips.
Leave them to crystallize briefly and then serve or store them in a cool place (18 °C) in a closed plastic container to keep them crispy.

TIP ⟶ *Experiment with other flavors of potato chips that fit the taste profile of the chocolate that you use.*

Blue cheese millefeuille

A French classic pâtisserie "le Millefeuille," but here made from Uganda 80% dark chocolate and filled with a creamy blue cheese filling. The perfect pairing: a stout like Lupulus Hibernatus.

COMPONENTS
For approximately 30 servings
Chocolate thin squares
Blue cheese filling

CHOCOLATE AND BEER PAIRING

The roasted malt and coffee notes of Lupulus Hibernatus complement the bold flavors of blue cheese and thyme walnut filling. The robust cocoa flavors of Uganda 80% dark chocolate adds depth, creating a harmonious and rich taste.

INGREDIENTS

Chocolate thin squares
4 g/portion

Uganda 80% dark chocolate	300 g

Blue cheese filling
8 g/portion

cream cheese (Philadelphia)	125 g
blue cheese	125 g
fresh thyme	2 g
walnuts, roasted and chopped	20 g

PREPARATION

Chocolate thin squares
Heat the Uganda 80% dark chocolate to 50 °C and temper it to 29 °C on a marble slab.
Spread the chocolate very thinly between two guitar sheets.
Cut into squares using a pastry wheel cutter.
Leave to crystallize for 1 hour before removing the guitar sheets.
For the colored ones on top, see decoration technique, p. 56.

Blue cheese filling
Mix the cream cheese and the blue cheese in a blender and add some chopped fresh thyme.
Add the finely chopped walnuts and mix with a spatula.
Pipe the cheese filling between the thin chocolate squares and decorate with fresh herbs.
Make them immediately before serving, or prepare them an hour or two ahead and store them in the fridge at no more than 4 °C.

Salty apero bonbons

Have you ever tried a salty apero bonbon? Here's your chance! This eclectic mix delivers an unforgettable tasting experience, blending sweet, savory and spicy notes harmoniously with an intense cacao-forward chocolate, the Uganda 80% dark chocolate.

COMPONENTS

For 200 apero bonbons of 10 g
Tempering & molding
Hazelnut praliné 80% base
Dried meat filling
Wasabi peanut filling
Spicy rice cracker filling

CHOCOLATE AND BEER PAIRING

Gouden Carolus whiskey-infused beer's rich, malty, and whiskey notes complement the savory meat, the spicy wasabi or the crunchy rice crackers. Hazelnuts add nuttiness, while Uganda 80% dark chocolate provides depth, creating a complex and balanced flavor.

INGREDIENTS

Tempering & molding 3 g/bonbon

Uganda 80% dark chocolate	500 g

Hazelnut praliné 80% base

hazelnuts, peeled	450 g
hazelnuts, with peel	150 g
sugar	150 g
water	30 g
salt	2 g

Dried meat filling 7 g/bonbon

Parma ham or prosciutto	75 g
crispy fried onions	35 g
hazelnut praliné 80% base	200 g
ghee (concentrated butter)	15 g
Uganda 80% dark chocolate	75 g

PREPARATION

Tempering & molding

Heat the Uganda 80% dark chocolate to 47 °C and temper it to 29.4 °C on a marble slab.
Mold the pre-colored molds with the tempered chocolate and leave to crystallize for 1 hour.
For coloring the molds, see basic techniques: "coloring of chocolate molds" p. 50.
Mold: Chocolate World CW1217

Hazelnut praliné 80% base

Roast both types of hazelnuts in an oven at 165 °C for about 15 minutes.
Take them out of the oven and leave them to cool down on a silicone sheet.
Put the sugar in a pan and add the water.
Bring this to a boil and continue boiling until it becomes a blond caramel color.
When you have a caramel, pour this over the roasted hazelnuts and set aside to cool.
Sprinkle the salt on top.
When cooled, break into chunks and put them in a robot cutter.
Mix at medium speed to obtain a thick, semi-liquid paste.
Be sure not to overheat the praliné during the mixing process.
Transfer this hazelnut praliné to a small container and set aside for the next steps.
Store at room temperature.

Dried meat filling

Put the thin slices of the Parma ham on a silicone sheet on a baking tray.
Dry bake the ham in an oven at 90 °C for about 1 hour with dampers open.
Set the ham aside to cool.
Once cooled, put the dried ham and the crispy fried onions in a small robot cutter and mix until you have small pieces of around 2 mm.
Mix this with the hazelnut praliné base.
Heat the ghee and the chocolate to approximately 47 °C and add this to the ham and onions; mix with a spatula.
Pour the filling on a marble slab and temper the filling, like chocolate, to a temperature of 26 °C.
Pipe the dried meat filling into the chocolate molds and leave to crystallize.
To aid crystallization, you can put the filled molds in a fridge at 4 °C for about 5 minutes.
Once the filling is crystallized, remove the filled molds from the fridge and let sit at room temperature for at least 5 minutes.
Finish the salty apero bonbons with tempered Uganda 80% dark chocolate.
Unmold after crystallization and store the bonbons in a cool and dry place.

Wasabi peanut filling
7 g/bonbon

wasabi peanuts	120 g
dry roasted salty peanuts	50 g
hazelnut praliné 80% base	200 g
ghee (concentrated butter)	15 g
Uganda 80% dark chocolate	75 g

Wasabi peanut filling

Put the wasabi peanuts and the salty peanuts in a small robot cutter and mix until you have pieces of around 2 mm.
Mix this with the hazelnut praliné base.
Heat the ghee and the chocolate to approximately 47 °C and add to the base, mixing with a spatula.
Pour the filling on a marble slab and temper, like chocolate, to a temperature of 26 °C.
Pipe the wasabi peanut filling into the chocolate molds and leave to crystallize.
To aid crystallization, you can put the filled molds in a fridge at 4 °C for about 5 minutes.
Once the filling is crystallized, remove the filled molds from the fridge and let sit at room temperature for at least 5 minutes.
Close the salty apero bonbons with tempered Uganda 80% dark chocolate.
Unmold after crystallization and store the bonbons in a cool and dry place.

Spicy rice cracker filling
7 g/bonbon

spicy rice crackers	150 g
smoked spicy paprika powder	3 g
hazelnut praliné 80% base	200 g
ghee (concentrated butter)	15 g
Uganda 80% dark chocolate	75 g

Spicy rice cracker filling

Put the spicy rice crackers and the smoked paprika powder in a small robot cutter and mix until you have small pieces of around 2 mm.
Mix this with the hazelnut praliné base.
Heat the ghee and the chocolate to approximately 47 °C and add to the base, mixing with a spatula.
Pour the filling on a marble slab and temper, like chocolate, to a temperature of 26 °C.
Pipe the spicy rice cracker filling into the chocolate molds and leave to crystallize.
To aid crystallization, you can put the filled molds in a fridge at 4°C for about 5 minutes.
Once the filling is crystallized, remove the filled molds from the fridge and let sit at room temperature for at least 5 minutes.
Finish the salty apero bonbons with tempered Uganda 80% dark chocolate.
Unmold after crystallization and store the bonbons in a cool and dry place.

Choux stick chocolate beer dip

Serve the sauce at 40 °C with the crunchy baked spiced herbal choux sticks.

Treat yourself to a blend of fulfilling decadence with our cinnamon choux sticks. Dipped in a rich sweet or salted chocolate beer sauce, this treat is highlighted by the warming mocha and woody flavors of the Costa Rica 64% dark chocolate.

COMPONENTS

For 75 choux sticks
Cinnamon choux sticks
Sweet chocolate beer dip
Salty sweet chocolate beer dip

CHOCOLATE AND BEER PAIRING

Costa Rica 64% dark chocolate's complex notes of wood, olive, coffee, and licorice enhance the salty choux sticks, and its smooth, roasted flavors complement Gulden Draak Imperial Stout's rich, malty sweetness.

INGREDIENTS

Cinnamon choux stick
5 g/choux

semi-skimmed milk	150 g
water	150 g
sugar	10 g
salt	2 g
butter	110 g
pastry flour	165 g
eggs	300 g
sugar	100 g
cinnamon	5 g

Chocolate beer dip (sweet)
5 g/choux

Gulden Draak imperial stout	100 g
glucose (optional)	30 g
cream (35% fat)	50 g
Costa Rica 64% dark chocolate	200 g

Chocolate beer dip (salty sweet)
5 g/choux

Gulden Draak imperial stout	100 g
Costa Rica 64% dark chocolate	200 g
cream (35% fat)	50 g
sea salt	3 g
chili powder or tabasco	1 g

PREPARATION

Cinnamon choux stick

Sift the flour.
Combine the sugar (100 g) and the cinnamon.
Bring the milk, water, sugar (10 g), salt and butter to a boil.
Remove from the heat and add the sifted flour.
Mix with a spatula into a homogenous dough.
Return to the heat and reduce the heat to low.
mix the dough for 2 minutes with a spatula.
Transfer this mixture to a stand mixer and mix for 1 minute with a paddle attachment at medium speed.
Add the eggs gradually and, when finished, check the dough texture.
Pipe long strips onto a greased baking tray and sprinkle with the cinnamon-sugar mixture.
Bake at 170 °C in a convection oven for 5 minutes with dampers closed and 10 minutes with dampers open (timing may vary depending on your oven).
Set aside to cool and then cut into sticks of approximately 12 cm.

Chocolate beer dip (sweet)

Boil the beer with the glucose (optional) and add the cream.
Pour the hot beer on the chocolate and mix with a spatula to create a homogeneous emulsion.
Give it a short mix with an immersion blender.
Serve the sauce at 40 °C with the crunchy baked cinnamon choux sticks.

Chocolate beer dip (salty sweet)

For this sauce, you may substitute some salt and dried herbs for the sugar cinnamon mixture on the choux sticks before baking.

Boil the beer and pour over the chocolate.
Boil the cream and add the chili powder and salt.
Then pour the warm cream over the chocolate and mix with a spatula to create a homogeneous emulsion.
Give it a short mix with an immersion blender.

Taste Teasers

Chocolate vinaigrette

Delight your taste buds with our unique chocolate vinaigrette paired with a delectable blue cheese salad and a refreshing beer. The rich, savory flavors of blue cheese and walnuts harmonize perfectly with the unexpected sweetness of the chocolate.

COMPONENTS

For 8 bottles of 50 ml
Chocolate vinaigrette
Blue cheese nut salad

CHOCOLATE AND PEER PAIRING

Costa Rica 64% dark chocolate's rich, complex flavors go perfectly together with a chocolate vinaigrette with a blue cheese nut salad. Tripel D'Anvers' sweet, spicy notes combine perfectly with the chocolate's flavor profile.

INGREDIENTS

Chocolate vinaigrette
50 ml/serving

extra virgin olive oil	180 g
truffle oil (or black truffle flakes)	5 g
Costa Rica 64% dark chocolate	60 g
balsamic vinegar	50 g
water	150 g
sea salt	1 g
black pepper	1.5 g

Blue cheese nut salad
To serve 2

rocket salad	100 g
mixed lettuce	150 g
Roquefort blue cheese	120 g
blueberries	50 g
walnuts, roasted	50 g

PREPARATION

Chocolate vinaigrette
Combine the olive oil and the truffle oil and heat to 35 °C.
Heat the Costa Rica 64% dark chocolate to 40 °C and add the oil.
Add the balsamic vinegar and the water and mix with an immersion blender.
Season with the salt and black pepper.
Keep at room temperature until serving.

Blue cheese nut salad
Wash the rocket salad and the mixed lettuce with water.
Put both salads in a bowl and toss gently by hand.
Put the salad in a deep serving dish.
Break the Roquefort blue cheese into pieces.
Garnish the salad with the Roquefort blue cheese pieces, the blueberries and the roasted walnuts.
Add other ingredients or garnishes to taste.
Serve immediately with a small bottle of the chocolate vinaigrette.

Brie croquette and chocolate mayo

Discover our delicious panko brie cheese croquette, perfectly paired with a unique chocolate mayonnaise. Complemented by a Belgian ale with a citrus taste profile, this appetizer offers a delightful blend of textures and flavors.

TASTE TEASERS

COMPONENTS

For approximately 20 servings of 45 g
Molding
Brie cheese croquette
Chocolate mayonnaise

CHOCOLATE AND BEER PAIRING

Uganda 80% dark chocolate harmonizes rich cocoa and roasted notes with the creamy tang of brie cheese croquettes, enhanced by the unique, velvety texture of chocolate mayonnaise. Combine it with a Tripel Karmeliet beer for a sophisticated and indulgent culinary experience.

INGREDIENTS

Molding
6 g/serving

Uganda 80% dark chocolate	300 g

Brie cheese croquette
30 g/serving

brie cheese	500 g
egg white	100 g
salt	2 g
panko bread crumbs	100 g
black pepper	2 g

Chocolate mayonnaise
5 g/serving

eggs	50 g
extra virgin olive oil	200 g
Uganda 80% dark chocolate	75 g
water	70 g
lemon juice	30 g
sea salt	3 g
black pepper	2 g

PREPARATION

Molding

Heat the Uganda 80% dark chocolate to 47 °C and temper to 29.4 °C on a marble slab.
Mold the semi-sphere polycarbonate molds 5 cm in diameter with the tempered chocolate.
Leave to set at 16 °C with a relative humidity level below 60% for 1 hour before you unmold them.
Mold: Chocolate World CW2251

Brie cheese croquette

Choose a brie cheese that has a firm, not too soft texture.
Cut the Brie into cubes of approximately 25 g without removing the skin.
Loosen up the egg whites with a fork and add salt.
Mix the panko with the black pepper.
Coat the Brie cheese cubes with the egg whites and then the panko bread crumbs.
Ensure the cheese is perfectly covered.
Refrigerate until needed, up to a maximum of 3 days.
To serve, fry them for about 2 minutes in a fryer at 170 °C.
After frying, place them on paper towels for 30 seconds.
Serve them in the completed dish immediately, while still hot.

Chocolate mayonnaise

Break the eggs into a tall measuring cup and then add the oil on top.
Place an immersion blender all the way into the measuring cup and begin mixing, pulling the immersion blender up until you have a mayonnaise.
Heat the Uganda 80% dark chocolate to 40 °C.
Add the chocolate and water to the mayonnaise and mix again with the immersion blender until you have a homogeneous chocolate mayonnaise.
Add the lemon juice, salt and black pepper and mix in with a spatula.
Store the mayonnaise in a cool place until serving.

To serve: Dress a serving dish with small dot of chocolate mayonnaise and place a chocolate cup on top. Put some fresh dill in the chocolate cup to prevent melting. Place the fried Brie cheese croquette inside. Decorate with mini purple Shiso cress, a slice of lemon, and some dots of chocolate mayonnaise.

Spiced chocolate rasp and cod

Elevate your culinary creations with a sweet twist: grated spiced chocolate! Transform traditional dishes by replacing truffle or Parmesan cheese with rich, spiced chocolate. Perfect for adding a touch of chocolate emotion to any meal.

COMPONENTS

For 6 rasps
of approximately 85 g
6 cod starter dishes
Spiced chocolate rasp
Beer Hollandaise sauce
Cod starter dish

CHOCOLATE AND BEER PAIRING

Fourchette beer, mildly bitter and refreshing, combines with the delicate cod fish, enhanced by anise and clove in Uganda 80% dark chocolate rasp. This combination creates a harmonious balance of savory, spicy, and rich chocolate flavors.

INGREDIENTS

Spiced chocolate rasp (85 g/rasp)

Uganda 80% dark chocolate	450 g
Pure Prime Pressed Cocoa Butter	50 g
Himalaya salt	15 g
anise powder	5 g
clove powder	2 g
licorice sticks	6 pieces

Beer Hollandaise sauce (30 g/portion)

butter	60 g
Selection White Intense 31% chocolate	20 g
egg yolks	60 g
Fourchette beer	60 g
cayenne pepper	1 g
salt	2 g

Cod starter dish (30 g/portion)

shallots	1 piece
butter (82% fat)	25 g
samphire	120 g
Fourchette beer	25 g
fresh cod filet	300 g
butter (82% fat)	30 g
butter (82% fat)	30 g
salt	1 g
shrimp cracker with squid ink	6 pieces

PREPARATION

Spiced chocolate rasp

Heat the Uganda 80% dark chocolate and the cocoa butter to 47 °C and temper it to 29.4 °C on a marble slab.
Add the salt, anise powder and clove powder and mix with a spatula.
Pipe the chocolate into tube-shaped silicone molds as in the picture.
After a minute, the chocolate will start to crystallize, at which point you can place a licorice stick in the center. Leave to crystallize completely in a cool and dry place.
Unmold the spiced chocolate rasps and store them in a cool, dry place for serving as part of a dinner.
Use a microplane zester to grate this chocolate over a hot dish.

Beer Hollandaise sauce

Melt and clarify the butter. In a separate pan, melt the Selection White Intense 31% chocolate and, when melted, combine with the clarified butter.
Heat the egg yolks and the Fourchette beer to 82 °C while whisking continuously.
When the mixture starts to thicken a little, you have obtained the correct texture.
Now add the melted butter preparation and whisk until you have a smooth, homogeneous mixture.
Add the melted white chocolate, salt and cayenne pepper.
Keep warm in a Bain Marie until use.

Cod starter dish

Cut the shallots into brunoise of 4 mm.
Put some butter (25 g) in a pan, add the shallots and simmer for a minute.
Add the samphire and simmer for another minute.
Deglaze with the Fourchette beer. Keep warm until serving.
Cut the cod into six pieces of 50 g each and put some butter (30 g) in a pan.
Fry the cod for one minute on each side.
During the last minute, put the rest of the butter (30 g) in the pan and baste the cod with the butter.
Take the cod out of the pan, set aside on paper towels and sprinkle with a little salt.
In a deep plate, assemble the dish: first put some prepared samphire in the plate and top it off with a piece of cod. Top with some beer Hollandaise sauce and decorate with a shrimp cracker and small green leaves.

At the table: Grate some spiced chocolate rasp over the guests' plates.

Mains

Beernaise steak and shoestring fries

Introducing the Beernaise! A delightful twist on classic béarnaise sauce, crafted with beer, white chocolate, and cocoa butter. Perfectly paired with a juicy filet mignon and crispy shoestring fries, this recipe is a true culinary masterpiece.

MAINS

COMPONENTS

For 4 main dishes, each 355 g in total
Shoestring fries
Beernaise sauce
Spanish Angus filet mignon
Chocolate decoration

CHOCOLATE AND BEER PAIRING

Cornet Oaked Strong Blond's smooth, vanilla-oaked notes complement the robust, earthy flavors of Uganda 80% dark chocolate together with the steak. The creamy sweet acidity of Beernaise sauce balances the chocolate's bitterness, enhancing the savory steak.

INGREDIENTS

Shoestring fries
150 g/portion

potatoes, russet (or other)	1000 g
Pure Prime Pressed Cocoa Butter	1000 g
sea salt	3 g

Beernaise sauce
50 g/portion

fresh tarragon	3 g
egg yolk	40 g
Cornet Oaked strong blond beer	40 g
tarragon vinegar	20 g
salt	1 g
butter (82% fat)	50 g
Pure Prime Pressed Cocoa Butter	50 g
Selection White Intense 31% chocolate	10 g

PREPARATION

Shoestring fries

Peel the potatoes and slice with a mandoline into small strings of 2x2 mm.
Rinse the sliced potatoes with cold water a couple of times to clean and to remove the starch.
Dry the potato shoestrings on kitchen paper towels.
Heat the cocoa butter to 170 °C and fry the potato shoestrings, in small batches, for about 3 to 4 minutes until they are golden and crispy.
Drain on paper towels and keep warm until serving. Sprinkle with sea salt.

TIP ⟶ *You can use the cocoa butter multiple times; you can also save money by using a good-quality vegetable oil instead of cocoa butter.*

Beernaise sauce

Make the Beernaise sauce immediately before serving.
Slice the fresh tarragon very thinly.
Heat the egg yolk, the Cornet Oaked beer, the tarragon vinegar, the fresh tarragon and the salt, whisking constantly, to a temperature of 85 °C.
When you have reached 85 °C, add the soft butter and the cocoa butter and whisk, keeping it warm.
Add the Selection White Intense 31% chocolate and whisk until everything is smooth.
Add some extra salt or black pepper to taste.
Serve immediately in a preheated sauce boat.

Spanish Angus filet mignon
150 g/portion

Spanish Angus filet mignon	600 g
salt	3 g
black pepper	2 g
butter (82% fat)	50 g
butter (82% fat)	50 g
garlic clove	1
fresh rosemary	25 g

Spanish Angus filet mignon

Cut the filet mignon into steaks of 150 g each; make them square if possible.
Let the steaks rest for a while to warm up from fridge temperature.
Put some salt and black pepper on both sides.
Heat a cast iron steel pan on a gas stove and add the butter.
When the butter begins turning brown, put the steaks in the pan and fry them for 2 minutes on each side.
Add the other 50 g of butter, the garlic clove and the fresh rosemary.
Baste with the butter for about a minute.
Remove the steaks from the pan and let rest for 2 minutes before serving.

Chocolate decoration
5 g/portion

Uganda 80% dark chocolate	50 g
Selection Dark Ebony 96% chocolate (cocoa mass)	50 g

Chocolate decoration

Heat the Uganda 80% dark chocolate and cocoa mass to 47 °C and temper to 29.4 °C on a marble slab.
Spread the tempered chocolate out very thinly between two guitar sheets and cut into squares of 8 cm.
Leave to crystallize for 2 hours in a cool, dry place and unmold.
Using some gold powder and a stencil, decorate the chocolate with a bull's head logo.
When serving at the table, place a decorated chocolate square on each steak and let it melt before your guests' eyes.

Bacon onion melt bonbon

Ever tried a bacon-onion melt bonbon on a perfectly cooked sous-vide pork tenderloin? This main dish combines the richness of chocolate, beer, and meat on one plate, complemented by carrot and parsnip cream. Uganda 80% chocolate provides the perfect synergy. Bon appétit!

MAINS

COMPONENTS

For 40 bonbons of 30 g
6 main dishes
Tempering & molding
Bacon & fried onion
Salty hazelnut praliné
Sous-vide pork tenderloin
Beer sauce
Carrot & parsnip cream

CHOCOLATE AND BEER PAIRING

Rodenbach Classic's tart, fruity notes are complemented by pork tenderloin, finished with a Uganda 80% dark chocolate bacon melt. This adds smokiness, while salty hazelnut praliné provides a touch of sweetness, creating a balanced, savory flavor profile.

INGREDIENTS

Tempering & molding
10 g/bonbon

Uganda 80% dark chocolate	350 g
Selection Dark Ebony 96% chocolate (cocoa mass)	150 g
Pure Prime Pressed Cocoa Butter	25 g

Bacon & fried onion
12 g/bonbon

smoked bacon	400 g
crispy fried onions	200 g

Salty hazelnut praliné filling
8 g/bonbon

hazelnuts, peeled	300 g
sugar	50 g
water	10 g
salt	5 g
Selection Dark Ebony 96% chocolate (cocoa mass)	20 g
ghee (concentrated butter)	20 g

PREPARATION

Tempering and molding

Combine the Uganda 80% dark chocolate, the Selection Dark Ebony 96% chocolate and the cocoa butter, heat to 47 °C and temper to 29 °C on a marble slab.
Mold the pre-colored chocolate molds with the tempered chocolate and leave to crystallize for 1 hour.
For coloring the molds, see basic techniques: "coloring of chocolate molds", p. 50.
For this design you'll need to make a sticker stencil with a plotter.
Mold: Chocolate World CW12023 (or smaller mold of 4 cm diameter semi-sphere)

Bacon and fried onion

Cut the smoked bacon into small cubes of 5 mm.
Bake them until they render their fat and become crispy.
Set aside on paper towels to drain.
Put fried onion crisps and the baked bacon cubes into a bowl and stir to combine.
Fill the chocolate molds with the mixture to 2/3 and keep at hand for the next step.

Salty hazelnut praliné filling

Roast the hazelnuts at 165 °C for about 15 minutes and let them cool on a silicone sheet. In the meantime, make a blond caramel by boiling sugar and water.
Pour the caramel over the roasted nuts and leave to cool down. Sprinkle with salt.
Once hardened, break into chunks and mix in a robot cutter into a thick, semi-liquid paste, making sure it doesn't overheat.
Warm the Selection Dark Ebony cocoa mass and ghee to 45 °C and add this to the hazelnut paste. Temper the mixture to 26 °C on a marble table.
Pipe the salty hazelnut praliné over the bacon & fried onion filling, stopping at 2 mm from the edge. Leave to crystallize in the fridge for 5-10 min.
Finish with tempered Uganda 80% dark chocolate. Unmold after crystallization and store in a cool, dry place.

Sous-vide pork tenderloin
100 g/portion

clove of garlic	2 pieces
olive oil	50 g
branch of rosemary	2 pieces
branch of thyme	3 pieces
Dijon mustard	30 g
honey	20 g
salt	1 g
black pepper	1 g
pork tenderloins (+/- 350 g each)	700 g

Sous-vide pork tenderloin
Cut the cloves of garlic into big pieces.
Put all the ingredients except the pork tenderloins in a vacuum bag and massage the bag gently to mix everything.
Add the pork tenderloins and vacuum-seal the bags.
Sous-vide the bags at 58 °C in a water bath for 2 hours.
Before serving, remove the pork tenderloins from the vacuum bag and fry them with some butter in a hot pan until the outsides are just browned.
Cut into pieces 5 cm high and serve immediately.

Beer sauce
50 g/portion

shallots	30 g
butter 82% fat	20 g
olive oil	10 g
rodenbach classic Beer	250 g
veal stock	250 g
salt & pepper	as needed

Beer sauce
Finely dice the shallots and place them in a pot with the butter and olive oil.
Sauté the shallots until soft, then deglaze with the brown beer.
Reduce the beer by half through cooking.
Add the veal stock and reduce by two-thirds.
The sauce should have a syrup-like consistency.
Season with salt and pepper to taste.

Carrot & parsnip
80 g/portion

carrots	250 g
cream 20% fat	100 g
butter	40 g
salt	
parsnips	250 g
cream 20% fat	100 g
butter	40 g
salt	

Carrot & parsnip
Peel the carrots and steam them for 10 minutes until soft.
Bring 100 g of cream to a boil and add the steamed carrots.
Boil together for 2 minutes.
Transfer to a Thermomix and add 40 g of cold butter.
Blend on medium-high speed for about 3 minutes until smooth. Season with salt.
Peel the parsnips and steam them for 10 minutes until soft.
Bring 100 g of cream to a boil and add the steamed parsnips.
Boil together for 2 minutes.
Transfer to a Thermomix and add 40 g of cold butter.
Blend on medium-high speed for about 3 minutes until smooth. Season with salt.
Keep both warm for serving.

ASSEMBLY

Pipe some carrot and parsnip cream onto a warm serving plate and place a piece of pork tenderloin on top.
Add a few steamed baby carrots and some fresh greens.
At the table, place a bacon and onion bonbon on top of the meat and allow it to melt slightly.
Finish by pouring hot beer sauce over the dish.

Signature Desserts

Bababeer chocolate chantilly

Discover our delectable new creation: Bababeer, topped with a light lime milk chocolate chantilly cream and accented with the unique essence of Buddha's hand citron. This dessert promises a harmonious blend of flavors.

COMPOSITION

For 20 baba desserts of 90 g
Baba dough
Beer & liquor syrup
Milk chocolate chantilly
Chocolate decoration

CHOCOLATE AND BEER PAIRING

This baba dessert infused with Blanche De Namur beer offers a subtle, fruity tang. The topping of chantilly made from Vietnam 45% milk chocolate adds creamy, rich notes that beautifully balance the beer's flavors.

INGREDIENTS

Baba dough
20 g/baba

flour	200 g
sugar	10 g
milk	30 g
fresh yeast	10 g
eggs	120 g
salt	3 g
butter (82% fat)	60 g

Beer & liquor syrup
30 g/baba

Buddha's hand citrus slices (or lemon)	25 g
Blanche De Namur	350 g
water	300 g
sugar	350 g
glucose	30 g
Liquor Fleur de Bière 40%	50 g

Milk chocolate chantilly
35 g/baba

gelatin powder	2 g
water (to soak the gelatin)	12 g
cream (35% fat)	350 g
lime zest	3 g
Vietnam 45% milk chocolate	160 g
cream (35% fat)	150 g

PREPARATION

Baba dough
Mix all the ingredients except the butter together in a stand mixer with a paddle attachment for 8 minutes. Keep the dough at a maximum temperature of 22 °C.
Cover the bowl with a wet kitchen towel, keeping the towel from touching the dough, and let it rest at room temperature for 30 minutes.
Heat the butter to 35 °C and add it gradually to the dough while mixing again for about 12 minutes.
Pipe approximately 20 g per portion of the dough into silicone savarin molds of 4-5 cm in diameter.
Leave to proof for about 45 minutes at room temperature.
Bake the babas at 180 °C for about 20 minutes with dampers closed.
Unmold immediately after baking and set them aside to cool.

Beer and liquor syrup
Slice the Buddha's hand very thinly.
Boil the beer, water, sugar and glucose for 1 minute.
Add the slices of Buddha's hand, cover with cling film and leave to cool in a fridge at 4 °C.
When the syrup is cold, remove the slices of the Buddha's hand from the syrup and reserve for decoration and as an extra flavor component for the dessert.
Add the Liquor Fleur de Bière to the syrup and put the babas in it to soak.
Take the babas out of the syrup after 20 minutes and place them in serving cups.

Milk chocolate chantilly
Soak the gelatin powder in the cold water. Zest the lime finely using a microplane.
Bring the cream (350 g) to a boil with the lime zest and pour over the Vietnam 45% milk chocolate.
Add the soaked gelatin powder and mix with an immersion blender for 2 minutes.
Add the cold cream (150 g) and mix very briefly with the immersion blender.
Set aside in a fridge at 4 °C overnight.
Whip this chantilly cream in a stand mixer with a whisk to obtain a pipeable texture.
Be careful not to overwhip the cream.
Use immediately to decorate the soaked babas.

Chocolate decoration
5 g/baba

Vietnam 73% dark chocolate	200 g

Chocolate decoration

For the creation of this decoration, see p. 53.

ASSEMBLY

Put the soaked babas in a deep glass serving dish and place a disc of chocolate decoration on each. Pipe the chocolate chantilly on top and decorate with more chocolate decorations and some slices of the Buddha's hand.

Coco IPA beer dessert exotique

My goal here was to create a white chocolate beer dessert that would not be too sweet. This combination of Houblon Chouffe beer, mango, passion fruit, ginger and lemongrass is a well-balanced exotic creation complemented with Selection White Intense chocolate.

COMPONENTS

For 25 plated desserts of 120 g

Italian beer meringue
Coconut dacquoise
Mango beer chutney
Neutral beer glaze
Beer lemongrass mousse
Coconut beer glaze
Coconut sponge cake
Decorations

CHOCOLATE AND BEER PAIRING

A plated dessert featuring Houblon Chouffe beer sings with hoppy, citrusy note. Combined with white chocolate, mango, passion fruit, coriander, and coconut, it creates a tropical, creamy blend with a refreshing hint of spice and sweetness.

INGREDIENTS

Italian beer meringue
4 g/dessert

Houblon Chouffe beer	175 g
albumin (egg white powder)	25 g
sugar	200 g
water	40 g

PREPARATION

Italian beer meringue

Bring the beer to a boil briefly and set aside to cool down.
Mix the albumin powder and the beer and leave to rest for 5 minutes to allow the albumin powder to rehydrate.
Put this in a stand mixer with a whisk attachment, and whip until the texture is firm and meringue-like.
In the meantime, boil the sugar and the water at 118 °C.
Add this sugar syrup to the beer meringue while mixing at low speed, then turn the speed up again.
Whip until a firm meringue is obtained.
Pipe small peaks onto a silicone sheet and dry bake in an oven at 100 °C for 90 minutes with open dampers.
Store this prepared component in a dry place.

Coconut dacquoise
12 g/dessert

flour	30 g
icing sugar	150 g
almond powder pure	75 g
shredded coconut powder	75 g
egg white	150 g
sugar	85 g

Coconut dacquoise

Sift the flour and the icing sugar with the almond and coconut powder.
Whip the egg whites and the sugar until you have a firm meringue.
Fold the whipped egg white into the sifted ingredients gently with a spatula.
Pipe 40 circles of 5 cm diameter on a tray lined with baking paper and bake at 200 °C for 10 minutes with dampers closed.
Set aside to cool.
Use this dacquoise to create the dessert with the mousse.

Mango beer chutney
25 g/dessert

gelatin powder	6 g
water (to soak the gelatin)	36 g
sugar	50 g
pectin NH	6 g
Houblon Chouffe beer	100 g
diced fresh mango pieces	350 g
fresh passion fruit	50 g
fresh coriander leaves	5 g
white vinegar	5 g

Mango beer chutney
Add the gelatin powder to the cold water and leave to soak.
Combine the pectin and the sugar.
Heat the beer, the mango pieces and the passion fruit to 50 °C and add the pectin-sugar mixture.
Cook this for 3 minutes.
Add the soaked gelatin and mix with a spatula.
Cut fresh coriander leaves and add to the cooked fruit mixture with the vinegar.
Pour 25 g of the mango beer chutney into a half-sphere silicone mold of 4 cm diameter for each dessert and set aside in the freezer.

Neutral beer glaze
4 g/dessert

gelatin powder	4 g
water (to soak the gelatin)	24 g
sugar	30 g
pectin NH	10 g
Houblon Chouffe beer	150 g
water	50 g
sugar	150 g
glucose	150 g
lemon juice	5 g

Neutral beer glaze
Soak the gelatin powder in the cold water (24 g).
Combine the pectin and the sugar (30 g).
Heat the beer, the water (50 g), the sugar (150 g) and the glucose to 50 °C and add the sugar-pectin mixture while whisking.
Bring this to a gentle boil and skim off the foam with a spoon.
Boil for 2 minutes.
Add the lemon juice and the soaked gelatine, mix. Transfer to a bowl, cover in cling film, and set aside to cool.
When ready to glaze the mango beer chutneys, reheat the glaze to 30 °C and dip the frozen mango beer chutneys to coat.

Beer lemongrass mousse
40 g/dessert

cream (35% fat)	400 g
gelatin powder	6 g
beer (to soak the gelatin)	36 g
lemongrass	1 stick
ginger	6 g
cream (35% fat)	160 g
Selection White Intense 31% chocolate	360 g
Houblon Chouffe beer	120 g

Beer lemongrass mousse
Semi-whip the cream (400 g) and put aside.
Soak the gelatin in the cold beer.
Cut the lemongrass into small pieces and grate the ginger.
Boil the fresh cream (160 g) and infuse with the lemongrass and grated ginger for 30 minutes.
Boil again and strain out the lemongrass and ginger; then pour over the Selection White Intense 31% chocolate.
Bring the beer to a boil briefly and then add it to the mousse mixture.
Add the soaked gelatin and whisk.
When the ganache reaches 32 °C, incorporate the whipped cream using a spatula.
Use the mousse immediately.

Coconut beer glaze
15 g/dessert

gelatin	8 g
water (to soak the gelatin)	48 g
coconut puree	50 g
Houblon Chouffe beer	100 g
glucose	125 g
Selection White Intense 31% chocolate	250 g
miroir neutral glaze	250 g

Coconut beer glaze
Soak the gelatin in the cold water.
Boil the coconut puree, the Houblon Chouffe beer and the glucose.
Pour over the Selection White Intense 31% chocolate.
Mix with a spatula and add the melted pre-soaked gelatin.
Add the miroir neutral glaze and mix with an immersion blender.
Leave the glaze to cool overnight at room temperature.
Reheat to 37 °C before use and mix with an immersion blender to remove any air bubbles.
Glaze the frozen beer lemongrass mousses.

Coconut sponge cake
8 g/dessert

coconut cream (17% fat)	150 g
icing sugar	100 g
egg white	90 g
flour	30 g
coconut flour	20 g
vegetable oil	12 g
baking powder	5 g

Coconut sponge cake
Put all ingredients in a bowl and mix with an immersion blender.
Take paper coffee cups and poke some holes in the bottom.
Put 40 g of the sponge batter in each cup and microwave for about one and a half minutes at 850 watts.
Take out of the microwave and set the cups upside-down to cool.
Decorate the plated dessert with small pieces of the coconut sponge cake.

Decorations
5 g/dessert

Selection White Intense 31% chocolate	200 g
yellow fat-soluble coloring powder	4 g
fresh mango	as needed
Honny® cress leaves	as needed

Decorations
Heat the Selection White Intense 31% chocolate to 45 °C and add the yellow coloring powder.
Mix with an immersion blender.
Temper it to 28.5 °C and make the chocolate decorations (see p. 58, 60 & 61).
Remove the peel from the fresh mango and cut a slice 1 cm thick.
Cut out small circles of 1 cm diameter and use to decorate the plated dessert.
Wash the honey cress and use the leaves as a decoration and flavor addition to the plated dessert.

ASSEMBLY

Place 25 steel dessert rings 7 cm in diameter and 1.5 cm high on a tray lined with baking paper.
Put a coconut dacquoise on the bottom of each and fill with the beer lemongrass mousse.
Even it out with a spatula.
Put in the freezer and, when frozen, glaze with the coconut beer glaze.
Glaze the frozen mango beer chutneys with the neutral beer glaze.
Compose the plated dessert as in the picture, adding all the extra decorations wand textures from this recipe.

Grapefruit IPA raspberry delight

Indulge in a delightful fusion of flavors with this innovative recipe. A refreshing IPA grapefruit beer with an intense vanilla white chocolate, some raspberry, and a soft grapefruit almond cake create a truly exquisite and tangy dessert.

COMPONENTS

For 25 desserts of approximately 95 g
Almond grapefruit soft cake
Raspberry beer compôte
Beer grapefruit mousse
Neutral beer glaze
Crunchy raspberry coating
Chocolate decoration

CHOCOLATE AND BEER PAIRING

This dessert with Kerel grapefruit IPA delivers a zesty, bitter note. Paired with raspberry and white chocolate, it creates a vibrant, tangy blend with creamy sweetness, each flavor complementing the others for a refreshing experience.

INGREDIENTS

Almond grapefruit soft cake
15 g/dessert

grapefruit zest	15 g
almond powder	190 g
flour	50 g
eggs	120 g
sugar	100 g
Selection White Intense 31% chocolate	150 g
Kerel Grapefruit IPA beer	100 g
albumin (egg white powder)	15 g
sugar	70 g

Raspberry beer compôte
20 g/dessert

gelatin powder	6 g
water (to soak gelatin)	36 g
raspberries (frozen)	150 g
Kerel Grapefruit IPA	150 g
invert sugar	40 g
pectin NH	3 g
sugar	20 g

PREPARATION

Almond grapefruit soft cake
Zest a fresh grapefruit with a microplane zester.
Sift the almond powder and the flour together.
Whip the eggs with the sugar (100 g) in a stand mixer with a whisk at high speed.
In the meantime, heat the Selection White Intense 31% chocolate to 40 °C in a plastic bowl.
Put the whipped egg mixture on top of the melted white chocolate.
Whip the beer, the albumin powder and the sugar in the stand mixer with a whisk to obtain a firm beer meringue.
Combine the melted white chocolate and the whipped egg mixture with a spatula and add the flour, almond powder and grapefruit zest.
Finally, add the whipped beer meringue and fold in gently with a spatula.
Spread the moelleux cake batter on a tray of 30 x 40 cm and 1 cm thick.
Bake at 175 °C for about 16 minutes, depending on the oven, with dampers closed.
Remove from the oven and when the almond cake has cooled, cut out circles 5 cm in diameter.

Raspberry beer compôte
Soak the gelatine powder in the cold water.
Heat the raspberries, the Kerel Grapefruit IPA and the invert sugar to 50 °C.
Meanwhile, combine the pectin NH and the sugar.
Once the raspberry mixture reaches 50 °C, add the sugar-pectin mixture.
Bring to a boil while whisking, and cook for 2 minutes at medium heat.
Remove from the heat and add the soaked gelatin.
Cool the mixture, stirring, until it reaches 50 °C.
Fill silicone molds with 20 g per portion and place in the freezer.
Mold: Silikomart SF186

Beer grapefruit mousse
30 g/dessert

gelatin powder	4 g
water (to soak gelatin)	24 g
cream (35% fat)	300 g
cream (35% fat)	110 g
Papua New Guinea 36% white chocolate	270 g
Kerel Grapefruit IPA beer	75 g
grapefruit juice	35 g

Beer grapefruit mousse
Soak the gelatine powder in the cold water.
Semi-whip the cream (300 g) until it forms soft peaks.
Bring the cream (110 g) to a boil and pour over the Papua New Guinea 36% white chocolate, mixing with a spatula.
Bring the Kerel Grapefruit IPA to a gentle boil and add the grapefruit juice.
Add this to the chocolate and continue mixing with a spatula.
Add the soaked gelatin and keep mixing with a spatula to obtain a ganache texture.
When the ganache reaches a temperature of 35 °C, you can add the semi-whipped cream in two stages, mixing gently with a spatula each time.

Neutral beer glaze
12 g/dessert

gelatin powder	10 g
water (to soak the gelatin)	60 g
sugar	30 g
pectin NH	10 g
Kerel Grapefruit IPA	150 g
water	150 g
sugar	150 g
glucose	150 g
lemon juice	5 g

Neutral beer glaze
Soak the gelatin powder in the water (60 g).
Combine the pectin and the sugar (30 g).
Heat the beer, water (150 g), sugar (150 g) and glucose to 50 °C.
Add the sugar-pectin mixture while whisking.
Bring this to a gentle boil and skim off the foam with a spoon.
Boil for 2 minutes.
Remove from the heat and add the soaked gelatine.
Add the lemon juice, transfer to a bowl, cover with cling film and set aside to cool.
When ready to glaze, reheat to 32 °C.

Crunchy raspberry coating
12 g/dessert

almond cubes (2 mm, or small pieces)	50 g
Papua New Guinea 36% white chocolate	400 g
grapeseed oil (or other neutral oil)	40 g
freeze-dried raspberry pieces	20 g

Crunchy raspberry coating
Roast the almond cubes and leave to cool.
Heat the Papua New Guinea 36% white chocolate to 40 °C and add the grapeseed oil.
Mix with a spatula.
Add the other ingredients and mix with a spatula again.

Chocolate decoration
4 g/dessert

Selection White Intense 31% chocolate	200 g

Chocolate decoration
Heat the Selection White Intense 31% chocolate to 45 °C and temper it to 28.5 °C on a marble slab.
Make the chocolate decorations.
Spread out the chocolate between 2 guitar sheets (p. 52) and cut out circles with dough cutters.
Leave to crystallize and then unmold to decorate the dessert.

ASSEMBLY

Pipe some beer grapefruit mousse on top of the frozen raspberry beer compote and finish with a slice of the almond grapefruit soft cake. Freeze. After freezing, dip just the top of the dessert in the neutral beer glaze coating only the raspberry beer compote and put back in the freezer. Dip the bottom and sides of the dessert in the raspberry coating. Place on a baking sheet to let the coating set and defrost. Decorate with the chocolate decoration.

Chocolate tripel hoppy

A creation that is close to my heart, one of the first beer and chocolate creations I ever developed. A very nice combination of flavors with lots of different textures: salty peanuts, crispy corn, orange, hops and Vietnam 45% milk chocolate.

COMPONENTS

For 30 desserts of 110 g
Salty peanut crisp
Almond dacquoise
Orange marmalade
Beer chocolate mousse
Beer chocolate glaze

CHOCOLATE AND BEER PAIRING

The Duvel Tripel Hop Citra Belgian IPA brings citrusy, hoppy notes to this dessert. Combined with Vietnam 45% milk chocolate, peanuts, and cornflakes, it creates a rich, nutty, and crunchy blend with a refreshing orange twist.

INGREDIENTS

Salty peanut crisp
20 g/portion

almonds, peeled	140 g
sugar	50 g
Vietnam 45% milk chocolate	120 g
cornflakes, crushed	195 g
salted peanuts, broken	150 g
sea salt	3 g

Almond dacquoise
15 g/portion

egg white	270 g
sugar	330 g
almond powder	195 g
icing sugar	135 g
diced almond	100 g

Orange marmalade
15 g/portion

fresh oranges	350 g
glucose	90 g
sugar	20 g
pectin NH	4 g

TIP ⟶ If you don't have a Thermomix, you can also blend the oranges in a blender into a thick juice before you start cooking the marmalade.

PREPARATION

Salty peanut crisp
Roast the almonds and leave them to cool on a silicone sheet.
Dry caramelize the sugar and pour over the roasted almonds.
Set aside to cool.
Grind this almond-sugar mixture in a blender to obtain an almond praliné.
Heat the Vietnam 45% milk chocolate to 40 °C and add the almond praliné.
Add the crushed cornflakes, salted peanuts and salt.
Mix with a spatula.
Put 20 g of the crisp in rings 5 cm in diameter and smooth it with a spoon.
Freeze and unmold.

Almond dacquoise
Whip the egg whites, then gradually add the sugar and keep whipping until firm.
Sift all other dry ingredients together and fold gently into the whipped meringue with a spatula.
Spread on a baking tray of 40 x 60 cm and sprinkle the diced almond on top (to minimize waste, you can also pipe circles of the dacquoise instead).
Bake at 200 °C for 10 minutes with closed dampers and set aside to cool.
Cut out circles of 5 cm (60 pieces).

Orange marmalade
Wash the oranges and segment them, removing the seeds but keeping on the peels.
Cut the orange fruit flesh into large chunks (keeping the peel on).
Cook and blend the orange pieces with the glucose in a Thermomix.
Combine the sugar and the pectin NH.
When the orange pieces are warm, add the pectin and sugar mixture.
Boil for 3 minutes at low speed in the Thermomix.
Set aside to cool.
Pipe 10 g of this marmalade between two dacquoise circles.
Set this component aside in the freezer.

Beer chocolate mousse
40 g/portion

cream (35% fat)	600 g
Duvel Trippel Hop Citra (to soak the gelatin)	48 g
gelatin powder	8 g
Duvel Trippel Hop Citra	120 g
sugar	60 g
egg yolks	120 g
Vietnam 45% milk chocolate	190 g
Selection Dark Intense 65% chocolate	110 g
cream (35% fat)	75 g

Beer chocolate mousse

Semi-whip the cream (600 g).
Bring the Duvel beer (48 g) to a gentle boil and set aside to cool.
Soak the gelatin powder in the cooled beer (48 g).
Heat the beer (120 g), sugar and egg yolks to 85 °C.
Put the warm beer-egg yolk mixture in a whipping machine and whip until very aerated and lukewarm.
Heat the Vietnam 45% milk chocolate and the Selection Dark Intense 65% chocolate to 45 °C.
Melt the soaked gelatin.
Add the cream (75 g) to obtain a ganache and then add the melted gelatin.
Place the warm beer and egg yolk mixture in a whipping machine and whip until light, airy, and lukewarm.
Melt the Vietnam 45% milk chocolate and Selection Pure Intense chocolate together until they reach 45 °C (113 °F).
Melt the pre-soaked gelatin.
Add 75 g of cream to the melted chocolate to create a ganache, then stir in the melted gelatin.
Gently fold the whipped beer and egg yolk mixture into the ganache using a spatula.
Finally, fold in the semi-whipped cream and use the mousse immediately.

Beer chocolate glaze
20 g/portion

Duvel Trippel Hop Citra beer (to soak gelatin)	90 g
gelatin powder	15 g
Duvel Trippel hop Citra beer	150 g
glucose	250 g
Vietnam 45% milk chocolate	400 g
miroir neutral glaze	500 g

Beer chocolate glaze

Bring the Duvel Trippel Hop Citra (90 g) to a gentle boil and set aside to cool.
Soak the gelatin powder in the cooled beer (90 g).
Bring the Duvel Trippel Hop Citra (150 g) and the glucose to a boil.
Pour over the Vietnam 45% milk chocolate and add the pre-soaked gelatin.
Mix into the ganache.
Add the miroir neutral glaze and mix everything with an immersion blender.
Leave the glaze to cool overnight to room temperature.
Reheat and use at 38 °C.
Mix with an immersion blender to remove air bubbles before use.

ASSEMBLY

Place 30 steel rings 6 cm in diameter and 4 cm high on a guitar sheet on a tray.
Put some chocolate mousse in each ring and smooth it with a spatula.
Press the 2 dacquoise sponges filled with the orange marmalade into the mousse.
Add more chocolate mousse and cover with the peanut crisps.
Freeze the beer desserts until frozen.
Unmold and glaze the desserts with the beer chocolate glaze.
Sprinkle some gold color on the glaze.
Decorate with chocolate decorations (see p. 59).

Chocolate beer glass dessert

I couldn't resist creating a dessert inspired by the shape of a beer glass. This treat features layers of beer textures, apricot and white chocolate, and is topped with frozen beer foam that melts delightfully on your tongue.

COMPONENTS

For 30 desserts of 92 g
Beer pistachio moelleux cake
Beer apricot cream
White chocolate chantilly
Frozen beer foam
Yellow chocolate tube

CHOCOLATE AND BEER PAIRING

The Vedett IPA adds hoppy and citrusy notes. Combined with vanilla and anise flavors from Papua New Guinea 36% white chocolate, the apricot and almond sponge creates a fruity and nutty blend.

INGREDIENTS

Beer pistachio moelleux cake
15 g/dessert

almond powder	100 g
pistachio powder	90 g
flour	50 g
eggs	120 g
sugar	100 g
Selection White Intense 31% chocolate	150 g
Vedett IPA Beer	100 g
Albumin (egg white powder)	15 g
Sugar	70 g

Beer apricot cream
15 g/dessert

gelatin powder	3 g
water (to soak the gelatin)	18 g
Vedett IPA	130 g
apricot puree	60 g
sugar	40 g
eggs	80 g
egg yolk	20 g
butter 82% fat	100 g

PREPARATION

Beer pistachio moelleux cake
Sift the almond powder, pistachio powder and flour together.
Whip the eggs with the sugar (100 g) in a stand mixer with a whisk at high speed.
In the meantime, heat the Selection White Intense 31% chocolate to 40 °C in a bowl.
Add the whipped egg mixture to the white chocolate.
In the stand mixer, whisk the Vedett IPA, albumin powder and sugar (70 g) until you have a firm beer meringue.
Fold the whipped egg mixture into the melted white chocolate with a spatula and add the flour, almond powder and pistachio powder.
Finally, add the whipped beer meringue and mix with a spatula until smooth.
Spread the moelleux cake batter on a tray of 30 x 40 cm in a layer 1 cm thick.
Bake at 175 °C for about 16 minutes, depending on your oven, with dampers closed.
Set the moelleux cake aside and, when cooled, cut out circles 5 cm in diameter.

Beer apricot cream
Soak the gelatin powder in the cold water.
Put the Vedett IPA in a pan and add the apricot puree, sugar, eggs and egg yolk.
Heat this mixture to boiling point while whisking constantly.
When the mixture begins to bubble, stop the heating process.
Add the soaked gelatin and set this mixture aside to cool until it reaches 40 °C.
When the mixture reaches 40 °C, add the cold butter in small cubes and mix for a minute with an immersion blender.
Set the beer apricot cream aside until plating the dessert.

White chocolate chantilly
30 g/dessert

gelatin powder	5 g
water (to soak the gelatin)	30 g
orange peel	10 g
cream (35% fat)	500 g
Selection White Intense 31% chocolate	270 g
cream (35% fat)	250 g

Frozen beer foam
20 g/dessert

gelatin powder	8 g
water (to soak the gelatin)	48 g
Vedett IPA	250 g
sugar	30 g
invert sugar	30 g

Yellow chocolate tube
12 g/dessert

Pure Prime Pressed Cocoa Butter	as needed
yellow fat-soluble coloring powder	2 g
Selection White Intense 31% chocolate	300 g

White chocolate chantilly

Soak the gelatin powder in the cold water.
Zest the orange with a microplane.
Bring the cream (500 g) to a boil with the orange peel.
Pour this over the Selection White Intense 31% chocolate and add the soaked gelatin.
Mix with an immersion blender for a minute.
Add the cold cream (250 g) and give it another short mix with the immersion blender.
Set aside to cool overnight in a fridge to be whipped the day after.
When ready to serve the dessert, whip the chantilly in a stand mixer with a whisk until soft peaks form.

Frozen beer foam

Soak the gelatin powder in the cold water.
Bring the Vedett IPA and the sugar to a boil.
Put the soaked gelatin and the invert sugar in the bowl of a stand mixer fitted with the whisk.
Add the warm beer mixture and start to whip at high speed.
The mixture will cool down while mixing and become very foamy.
In the meantime, set a steel frame 3 cm high (20 x 30 cm) in the freezer on a tray (put a guitar sheet in the tray first).
Put the foam in the frame and then place in the freezer.
When frozen, cut circles of 5 cm diameter.

Yellow chocolate tube

Melt the cocoa butter to 35 °C.
Put some yellow coloring powder on a guitar sheet and spread it out with the cocoa butter using a brush or a paint roller.
Move the brush from left to right to create yellow lines.
When the cocoa butter is dry you can stop brushing/painting.
Heat the Selection White Intense 31% chocolate to 45 °C and temper it to 28.5 °C on a marble slab.
Spread out the tempered chocolate over the colored guitar sheet.
Leave to set for a minute until dry to the touch.
Cut the chocolate to the desired width and put a sheet of baking paper on top.
Roll this around a plastic tube 5 cm in diameter and leave to crystallize.
Unmold the yellow-colored chocolate tubes and use them as a mold to create the dessert.

ASSEMBLY

Place the yellow chocolate tubes on serving dishes.
Add a layer of beer pistachio moelleux cake on the bottom and pipe some beer apricot cream on top.
During apricot season, you can always add some juicy fresh apricot (chopped) in the middle of the dessert.
Whip the chocolate chantilly, fill the tubes, and even the top with a spatula.
Just before serving, add frozen beer foam on top.

Gluten-free moelleux

Enjoy our gluten-free moelleux, crafted with premium Peru 64% dark chocolate and combined with Rodenbach Caractère Rouge. Dive into this crispy yet decadent delight.

SIGNATURE DESSERTS

(only the moelleux)

COMPONENTS

For 7 moelleux of 70 g
Moelleux
White chocolate beer chantilly
Crispy dentelle with beer
Beer coulis
Chocolate decoration

CHOCOLATE AND BEER PAIRING

Rodenbach Caractère Rouge offers tart, fruity notes. When paired with a moelleux made from Peru 64% dark chocolate, this dessert is a rich, dark chocolate experience with a refreshing, berry-like contrast.

INGREDIENTS

Moelleux
70 g/portion

egg	100 g
egg yolks	40 g
sugar	100 g
butter (82% fat)	100 g
Peru 64% dark chocolate	100 g
gluten-free flour mix	70 g

TIP ⟶ *You can also replace the gluten-free flour mix with regular patisserie flour.*

White chocolate beer chantilly
30 g/portion

gelatin powder	3 g
water (to soak the gelatin)	18 g
Rodenbach Caractère Rouge	100 g
Papua New Guinea 36% white chocolate	125 g
anise powder	1 g
cream (35% fat)	250 g

PREPARATION

Moelleux
Use fresh eggs.
Whip the eggs, egg yolks and sugar in a stand mixer with a whisk until fluffy.
In the meantime, heat the butter with the Peru 64% dark chocolate to approximately 40 °C.
Using a spatula, add the melted chocolate butter to the whipped eggs and sugar.
Sift the gluten-free flour mix into this mixture.
Mix with a spatula to obtain a homogenous moelleux batter.
Place steel rings 5 cm in diameter and 5 cm high on a baking tray with a silicone sheet underneath.
Put a strip of baking paper 5 cm high in each ring so you can unmold the moelleux easily after baking.
Pipe 70 g of the moelleux batter into each ring and bake for 4-5 minutes at 230 °C with dampers closed.
Remove from the oven and leave to set for 1 minute before unmolding.
Serve immediately.

White chocolate beer chantilly
Soak the gelatin powder in the cold water.
Bring the Rodenbach Caractère Rouge to a boil, and as soon as it reaches boiling point pour over the Papua New Guinea 36% white chocolate and the anise powder.
Heat the cream to 80 °C and add this to the mixture.
Mix briefly with an immersion blender and put in the fridge to chill overnight.
Just prior to serving the dessert, whisk the chantilly and pipe it onto the moelleux.

TIP ⟶ *To ensure the chantilly maintains its texture, make sure the moelleux is cooled slightly but still warm in the center.*

Crispy dentelle with beer
12 g/portion

butter (82% fat)	65 g
Rodenbach Caractère Rouge	75 g
brown sugar	200 g
gluten-free flour mix	25 g
Premium Dutch Cocoa Powder	10 g

Crispy dentelle with beer

Bring the butter, beer and brown sugar to a boil.
Sift the dry ingredients and add them.
Mix with a spatula until smooth and place in the fridge to set.
Pipe small dots on a silicone sheet with some distance between them, and bake at 160 °C for about 8 minutes (depending on the oven).
When cooled, store them in a sealed plastic container.
Keep in a dry place until needed for serving the dessert.

Beer coulis
30 g/portion

sugar	25 g
pectin NH	6 g
Rodenbach Caractère Rouge	350 g
sugar	50 g
glucose	100 g
citric acid	1 g
(or lemon juice 5 g)	

Beer coulis

Combine sugar (25 g) and pectin.
Heat the beer, sugar (50 g) and glucose to 50 °C and add the pectin-sugar mixture.
Add the citric acid crystals (or lemon juice).
Boil at 102 °C, whisking continuously.
Set aside to cool in a bowl covered with cling film.

Chocolate decoration
5 g/portion

Peru 64% dark chocolate	200 g

Chocolate decoration

For making the decoration, see p. 62.

ASSEMBLY

Place a moelleux, while still warm on the inside, on a serving tray and scoop some beer coulis around it.
Decorate with some cherry blossom flowers.
Pipe some beer chantilly on top and decorate immediately with a crispy dentelle.
Add the chocolate decoration and serve immediately.

Lactose-free pre-dessert lychee beer sorbet

A refreshing pre-dessert of an Old Geuze Granita with a beer-lychee sorbet. The combination of the Philippines 68% dark chocolate is just amazing. Are you ready for a pre-dessert like you've never had before?

COMPONENTS

For approximately 20 pre-desserts of 104 g

Lychee beer sorbet
Old Geuze beer granita
Beer meringue
Tuille leaves
Chocolate beer bottle and decoration

CHOCOLATE AND BEER PAIRING

Boon Oude Geuze beer adds tart, complex notes that cleanse the palate. Combined with Philippines 68% dark chocolate's rich, dark exotic flavor, the lychee and beer sorbet creates a refreshing fruit twist for the chocolate contrast.

INGREDIENTS

Lychee beer sorbet
35 g/portion

cocoa nibs	75 g
water	150 g
sugar	50 g
sorbet stabilizer powder	5 g
Boon Old Geuze beer	165 g
lychee puree juice	300 g
glucose powder (or normal glucose)	30 g
invert sugar	20 g

PREPARATION

Lychee beer sorbet

Soak the cocoa nibs overnight in cold water (150 g).
Strain out the cocoa nibs and re-weigh the water.
Add some extra water to obtain the same weight as at the beginning (150 g).
Combine the sugar and the sorbet stabilizer powder.
Bring the beer to a gentle boil for a minute and add the lychee puree.
Heat this to 50 °C and add the sugar/sorbet stabilizer mixture while mixing with an immersion blender.
Add the glucose powder and the invert sugar.
Heat to 85 °C, remove from the heat and add the cold-infused cocoa nib water.
Mix with the immersion blender again.
Leave to rest overnight in a fridge at 4 °C.
Process the sorbet in an ice cream maker.
Pipe the sorbet into silicone quenelle molds, smoothing with a spatula for a perfect fill.

TIP ⟶ *You can keep the sorbet in the freezer and make a scoop of sorbet afterwards. You can make your own lychee puree by peeling fresh lychees, removing the seeds and mixing the fruit with lychee puree juice.*
The sorbet stabilizer powder improves the shelf life; if you make the sorbet and use it right away, you can leave this ingredient out.

Old Geuze beer granita
30 g/portion

fresh pineapple (yellow quality)	300 g
Boon Old Geuze beer	300 g
lemon juice	30 g

Old Geuze beer granita

Remove the peel from a fresh pineapple.
In a blender, blend the fresh pineapple into a puree or juice.
Bring the Boon Old Geuze beer to a gentle boil briefly and then add the pineapple puree and the fresh lemon juice.
Transfer this mixture to a plastic container and place in the freezer.
Every 30 minutes, mix with a fork, breaking up the ice crystals each time.
After repeating this three or four times, your granita will have the right texture to serve.

Beer meringue
10 g/portion

Belgian IPA (any brand)	175 g
Albumin (egg white powder)	25 g
sugar	200 g
water	40 g

Beer meringue

Bring the beer to a boil briefly and set aside to cool down.
Mix the albumin powder and the beer and leave to rest for 5 minutes to allow the albumin powder to rehydrate.
Whisk in a stand mixer until it reaches a firm meringue texture.
In the meantime, boil the sugar and the water at 118 °C.
Add this sugar syrup to the beer meringue, mixing at lower speed at first before turning the speed up again.
Whip until a stiff meringue is obtained.
Spread the beer meringue on a sheet of baking paper on a baking tray and dry bake in an oven at 100 °C for 90 minutes with dampers open.
Break the beer meringue and store it in a dry place until needed.

Tuille leaves
4 g/portion

butter (82% fat) (lactose-free)	75 g
icing sugar	75 g
egg white	60 g
flour	75 g
salt	1 g
vanilla	1 g

Tuille leaves

Use the butter at room temperature and soften it in a stand mixer with the paddle attachment.
Sift the icing sugar and add it to the softened butter.
Add the egg white, flour, salt and vanilla.
Continue mixing at medium speed.
If the tuille batter splits, this means it's too cold and you'll need to heat it a bit with a heating gun on the side of the bowl while mixing.
Spread the tuille batter in specially designed silicone stencils and bake at 165 °C for about 6 minutes.
Remove from the oven and unmold immediately. Place them in a metal gutter to bend them a bit.
Set the tuille leaves aside to cool.
Store them in a closed box away from humidity.

TIP ⟶ *Mix this tuille batter gently without incorporating too much air; otherwise, the tuilles become too fragile to demold.*

Chocolate beer bottle and decoration
35 g/portion

Philippines 68% dark chocolate	as needed
fresh lychee	as needed
mint leaves	as needed

Chocolate beer bottle and decoration

Heat the Philippines 68% dark chocolate to 47 °C and temper to 29.4 °C.
Mold the half-bottle shaped molds and leave to crystallize for at least one hour at 16 °C with a relative humidity below 60%.
Unmold and use them to serve the pre-dessert.
Spread tempered Philippines 68% chocolate between two guitar sheets (see p. 52) and leave to crystalize.
Break this chocolate into medium-sized pieces.

ASSEMBLY

Put half a chocolate bottle on a cold serving plate.
For the first layer, put some Boon Old Geuze beer granita in the bottle and sprinkle some beer meringue pieces over it.
Immediately add a quenelle of the lychee beer sorbet on top.
Decorate with some broken chocolate pieces, fresh lychees, fresh mint leaves and, finally, a "tuille" leaf on top.
Serve immediately and enjoy.

Plant-based banabeer hazelnut

A plant-based plated dessert with hazelnut and fresh banana combined with a smooth touch of beer that goes well with this milk-alike Selection M. Plant-Based 46% chocolate. This creation combines the sensory experience of different textures like crunchy, aerated and creamy.

COMPONENTS

For 20 plated desserts of 105 g
Chocolate banana cake
Liquid beer hazelnut praliné
Plant-based beer chocolate mousse
Beer chocolate glaze
Aerated chocolate and decoration

CHOCOLATE AND BEER PAIRING

Chimay Blue beer adds rich, malty notes that complements the Selection M. Plant-Based chocolate's deep, cocoa flavor. Combined with banana and hazelnuts. It creates a creamy, nutty, and fruity vegan dessert.

INGREDIENTS

Chocolate banana cake
25 g/portion

fresh banana	350 g
Selection M. Plant-Based 46% chocolate	100 g
Pure Prime Pressed Cocoa Butter	25 g
hazelnuts, peeled & roasted	75 g
vegetable oil	120 g
hazelnut powder	250 g
icing sugar	300 g
baking soda	15 g
flour	220 g

Liquid beer hazelnut praliné
15 g/portion

hazelnuts, peeled & roasted	225 g
sugar	150 g
Chimay Blue	100 g

PREPARATION

Chocolate banana cake
Peel the bananas and blend into a smooth paste with a robot cutter or an immersion blender.
Melt the Selection M. Plant-Based 46% chocolate with the cocoa butter.
Mix the hazelnuts into a liquid paste with a robot cutter.
Add the oil to the hazelnut liquid paste and mix with a spatula.
Combine the hazelnut powder, icing sugar, baking soda and flour and add to the paste.
Then add the melted Selection M. Plant-Based 46% chocolate and cocoa butter.
Whisk until homogeneous and spread on a 30 x 40 cm tray covered with a sheet of baking paper.
Bake at 165 °C for about 20 minutes with dampers closed.
When cooled, cut into rectangles 3 cm wide at the length of the silicone mold that you will fill with the mousse.

TIP ⟶ *The mold I use for this cake comes with an oval-shaped dough cutter. If this recipe makes more cake than needed, you can freeze the remainder.*

Liquid beer hazelnut praliné
Roast the hazelnuts and leave them to cool on a silicone sheet.
Dry caramelize the sugar and pour over the roasted hazelnuts; set aside to cool.
Mix this in a robot cutter into a thick liquid paste.
Bring the Chimay Blue to a gentle boil briefly and set aside to cool.
Once the beer has cooled, you can add it to the hazelnut praliné.
Add the beer all at once and mix with a spatula.
Pour this beer hazelnut praliné on a silicone sheet and spread it to a thickness of 5 mm.
Put this in the freezer and cut strips 5 mm wide at the length of the silicone mold that you will fill with the mousse.

Plant-based beer chocolate mousse
40 g/portion

plant-based cream (sweetened) (23% fat)	260 g
plant-based almond milk	75 g
Chimay Blue	150 g
Selection M. Plant-Based 46% chocolate	320 g

Plant-based beer chocolate mousse
Whip the plant-based cream with the almond milk until smooth and aerated.
Bring the Chimay Blue to a gentle boil briefly and pour over the Selection M. Plant-Based 46% chocolate.
Mix with a spatula to obtain a ganache.
Mix with an immersion blender to make it smooth.
When the ganache reaches a temperature of 35 °C, fold in the whipped plant-based cream with a spatula and mix gently.
Use the chocolate mousse immediately.
Fill silicone mold tubes with this mousse and place them in the freezer.
Unmold when frozen and glaze them with the beer chocolate glaze, see next step.

Beer chocolate glaze
15 g/portion

sugar	100 g
pectin NH	10 g
Chimay Blue	275 g
glucose	185 g
citric acid	1 g
Selection M. Plant-Based 46% chocolate	350 g

Beer chocolate glaze
Combine the sugar and the pectin.
Bring the beer to a gentle boil briefly and then add the glucose and citric acid.
Add the pectin-sugar mixture and the citric acid while the beer is at a temperature of at least 50 °C.
Bring everything to a boil and cook for 1 minute.
Pour over the Selection M. Plant-Based 46% chocolate and mix with an immersion blender.
Leave to cool and set overnight at room temperature.
Immediately before using, reheat to 35 °C and mix again with an immersion blender to remove air bubbles.

TIP ⟶ If the glaze is a bit thick, you can add some water to adjust the viscosity.

Aerated chocolate and decoration
10 g/portion

Selection M. Plant-Based 46% chocolate	250 g
Pure Prime Pressed Cocoa Butter	25 g
grapeseed oil (or other)	10 g

Aerated chocolate and decoration
Heat the Selection M. Plant-Based 46% chocolate and the cocoa butter to 45 °C and temper it at 32 °C.
Add the grapeseed oil and mix with a spatula.
Transfer to a Siphon® bottle and seal.
Charge the Siphon® bottle with two N_2O capsules and shake well.
Make small dots on a guitar sheet and press down with another sheet until the dots are 1 mm thick.
Allow to crystallize, unmold and cut out circles using a dough cutter.
To make chocolate lava stones, empty the Siphon® bottle into a plastic container and put the aerated chocolate in the freezer immediately.
When frozen, break the chocolate into pieces. For making the decoration, see p. 65.

ASSEMBLY

Place a piece of chocolate banana cake on a serving plate.
Put the glazed beer chocolate mousse on top, then a frozen strip of the liquid beer hazelnut praliné on top of that.
Decorate the sides with the aerated chocolate discs and some chocolate lava stones.
Pipe some leftover liquid beer praliné on the plate and decorate with extra half-hazelnuts and fresh Shiso cress.

Dame Beer Blanche

Introducing a twist on the classic Dame Blanche dessert: creamy beer ice cream topped with rich chocolate sauce and whipped vanilla cream. This unique blend of flavors offers a delightful treat for adventurous dessert lovers.

COMPOSITION

For 10 Dame Beer Blanches of 185 g
Chocolate crèmeux
Beer ice cream quenelles
Chocolate sauce
Whipped vanilla cream
Chocolate decoration

CHOCOLATE AND BEER PAIRING

Carolus Imperial Dark beer adds rich, malty notes with hints of caramel and spice to vanilla ice cream. Finished with Philippines 68% dark chocolate sauce, it creates a deep, dark chocolate flavor combination.

INGREDIENTS

Chocolate crèmeux
15 g/portion

cream (35% fat)	75 g
milk	30 g
glucose	75 g
Philippines 68% dark chocolate	75 g

Beer ice cream quenelles
105 g/portion

Carolus imperial stout	500 g
sugar	50 g
ice cream stabilizer (optional)	3 g
butter (82% fat)	100 g
full-fat milk	500 g
milk powder (optional)	40 g
egg yolks	120 g
salt	1 g
Papua New Guinea 36% white chocolate	100 g

PREPARATION

Chocolate crèmeux
Heat the cream, milk and glucose to 85 °C.
Pour over the Philippines 68% dark chocolate and mix with a spatula to obtain a ganache.
Mix with an immersion blender, making sure to avoid incorporating air bubbles.
Pipe the chocolate crèmeux into silicone sphere molds and freeze.
Unmold and store them in the freezer.

Beer ice cream quenelles
Bring the beer to a boil briefly and set aside.
Dry mix the sugar and the ice cream stabilizer.
Combine the butter, milk, milk powder, egg yolks and salt and heat to 85 °C.
Using an immersion blender, mix in the sugar stabilizer mixture and then add the boiled beer.
Blend this ice cream mixture for 5 minutes with an immersion blender. Add the Papua New Guinea 36% white chocolate and mix again for a minute with an immersion blender.
Transfer the beer ice cream to a bowl and cover with cling film.
Leave to mature overnight in a fridge at 4 °C.
Put the mixture in an ice cream machine or turbine and run the machine until it reaches the texture of creamy ice cream.
Put the ice cream in silicone quenelle molds and freeze.
Unmold the beer ice cream quenelles before use.

Chocolate sauce
30 g/portion

Philippines 68% dark chocolate	120 g
Selection Milk 35% chocolate	50 g
milk (or beer)	120 g

Whipped vanilla cream
25 g/portion

vanilla pod	1/3
sugar	15 g
cream (35% fat)	250 g

Chocolate decoration
10 g/portion

Philippines 68% dark chocolate	200 g

Chocolate sauce
Put the two chocolates in a bowl and add the milk.
Heat in the microwave in steps of 30 seconds.
Mix with a small whisk or spoon to obtain a smooth liquid ganache or sauce.
You can always adapt the texture by adding more or less chocolate.
Serve the sauce at a temperature of 50 °C.

Whipped vanilla cream
Remove the seeds from the vanilla pod.
Add the sugar and the vanilla seeds to the cream.
Whip the cream with a whisk until light and stable.
Keep the whipped cream aside for assembling the dessert.

Chocolate decoration
For making the decoration, see p. 63.

ASSEMBLY

Arrange three quenelles of the beer ice cream on a serving dish and put some small chocolate crèmeux spheres in between. Pipe some vanilla cream over the arrangement and top with a chocolate decoration.
Serve with warm chocolate sauce.

Cherry beer chocolate cake

Celebrate a festive moment with this amazing cherry beer chocolate cake with a variety of textures. The sweet and sour combination takes you to another level of happiness.

COMPONENTS

For three entremets 18 cm in diameter and 4 cm high
Soft chocolate sponge
Cherry beer cream
Philippines 68% dark chocolate mousse
Dark chocolate cherry beer glaze

CHOCOLATE AND BEER PAIRING

Timmermans Lambicus Kriek adds sour cherry notes to a chocolate mousse cake. It combines perfectly with Philippines 68% dark chocolate, known for its rich cocoa, exotic and slightly peppery flavor.

INGREDIENTS

Soft chocolate sponge
100 g/cake

eggs	300 g
sugar	225 g
Philippines 68% dark chocolate	190 g
butter	100 g
flour	50 g
baking powder	2 g
salt	1 g

Cherry beer cream
180 g/cake

gelatin powder	3 g
water (to soak gelatin)	18 g
eggs	55 g
egg yolk	40 g
sugar	40 g
cherry puree	80 g
Timmermans Lambicus Kriek beer	100 g
butter (82% fat)	115 g
pitted Amarena cherries (sour)	120 g

PREPARATION

Soft chocolate sponge
Whip the eggs and the sugar together until fluffy.
Heat the Philippines 68% dark chocolate and the butter to approximately 40 °C.
Sift the dry ingredients together.
Mix both compositions together with a spatula and add the sifted ingredients and the salt.
Gently mix with a spatula just until you obtain a homogeneous chocolate cake batter.
Spread the chocolate cake batter out on a baking tray of 40 x 30 cm with a silicone sheet or a sheet of baking paper.
Bake at 200 °C for 18 minutes with dampers closed.
Leave to cool and cut out circles 16 cm in diameter.

Cherry beer cream
Soak the gelatin powder in the cold water.
Whisk the eggs, egg yolks and sugar together, making sure not to incorporate too many air bubbles.
Combine the cherry puree and the cherry beer, bring to a boil briefly, and pour over the egg mixture.
Heat to approximately 85 °C while whisking continuously.
Add the pre-soaked gelatin mass and set aside to cool.
When the mixture reaches 37 °C, add the cold butter and mix in with an immersion blender.
Pour the cherry beer cream into round silicone molds (16 cm diameter) to make an insert (140 g per cake) and divide 40 g of sour Amarena cherries per cream circle.
Place in the freezer until frozen and unmold before use.

Philippines 68% dark chocolate mousse
240 g/cake

cream (35% fat)	425 g
Timmermans Lambicus Cherry	60 g
sugar	20 g
egg yolk	100 g
Philippines 68% dark chocolate	220 g
cream (35% fat)	75 g

Philippines 68% dark chocolate mousse
Semi-whip the cream (425 g) until it forms soft peaks.
Heat the cherry beer, sugar and egg yolks to 85 °C, whisking continuously, as if preparing a Sabayon.
Pour this mixture into a stand mixer and whip it further to obtain a light, fluffy texture at 45 °C.
In the meantime, heat the Philippines 68% dark chocolate to 45 °C and add 75 g of cream (still liquid).
Mix into a smooth ganache.
Gently add the "Pate à Bombe" with a spatula and, finally, incorporate the semi-whipped fresh cream.
Use this mousse immediately.

Dark chocolate cherry beer glaze
60 g/cake

Timmermans Lambicus Kriek beer (to soak the gelatin)	72 g
gelatin powder	12 g
Timmermans Lambicus Kriek beer	100 g
glucose	150 g
Philippines 68% dark chocolate	325 g
Premium Dutch Cocoa Powder	15 g
miroir neutral glaze	500 g

Dark chocolate cherry beer glaze
Bring the cherry beer (72 g) to a gentle boil and place in the fridge to cool.
Once cooled, add the gelatin powder and leave to soak.
Bring the cherry beer (100 g) and the glucose to the boil.
Pour this over the Philippines 68% dark chocolate and the cocoa powder and mix.
Add the pre-soaked and melted gelatin to the mixture.
Finally, add the miroir neutral glaze (30°) and mix with an immersion blender.
Leave to crystallize overnight at room temperature.
Reheat to 38 °C before use.

TIP ⟶ *You can put the leftover glaze in the freezer and keep it for another batch of entremets.*

ASSEMBLY

Put the steel entremet rings (18 cm diameter and 4 cm high) on a guitar sheet or plastic sheet on a tray.
Half-fill the rings with the Philippines chocolate mousse.
Place an insert of the cherry beer cream in the middle and put a disk of soft chocolate sponge on top.
Top with some extra chocolate mousse to close the entremet circles and smooth with a spatula.
Put the entremets in the freezer at -18 °C overnight.
Glaze each frozen cake with the chocolate cherry beer glaze.
Cut the chocolate sponge leftovers into cubes and dust them with icing sugar to use them for decorating the side.
Decorate the top with decoration made from dark chocolate (p. 54).

Sweet Retreat

Beer churros and chocolate dip

Experience the fusion of churros made with beer and dipped in rich Papua New Guinea 70% dark chocolate. This unique treat combines the light, crisp texture of churros with the deep, decadent flavor of premium origins chocolate.

SWEET RETREAT

COMPONENTS

For 25 churros of 30 g
Beer churros
Melted chocolate dip

CHOCOLATE AND BEER PAIRING

The roasted barley, coffee, and dark chocolate notes of Monk's Stout Dupont complement the rich fruity, nutty and honey flavors of the Papua New Guinea 70% dark chocolate dip, creating a delightful combination with churros and their hint of cinnamon.

INGREDIENTS

Beer churros
28 g churros & 2 g sugar

Monk's Stout Dupont	200 g
salt	1 g
sugar	20 g
butter	120 g
flour	150 g
eggs	250 g
sugar	200 g
cinnamon powder	5 g

PREPARATION

Beer churros
Bring the beer to a boil with the salt, sugar and butter.
Add the flour and mix with a spatula until you have obtained a homogeneous dough.
Add the eggs one by one, mixing with a spatula to incorporate.
You should obtain a stiff pipeable dough texture.
Put the dough in a piping bag.
Grease the electric churros baking machine with a bit of baking spray and bake at 200 °C (without frying in oil) for 4 minutes.
Mix the 200 g of sugar with the cinnamon powder.
When the churros are baked, take them out of the churros maker and sprinkle them with the cinnamon sugar.

TIP ⟶ *You can brush a bit of melted butter on the churros to make sure that the cinnamon sugar sticks better to the churros.*

INGREDIENTS

Melted chocolate dip
10 g/churro

Papua New Guinea 70% dark chocolate	250 g
grapeseed oil	20 g

PREPARATION

Melted chocolate dip
Heat the Papua New Guinea 70% dark chocolate to approximately 45 °C.
Add the grapeseed oil and mix.
Serve in a preheated porcelain cup.

Chocolate choux beer and crumble

Experience the exquisite harmony of flavors with our chocolate choux pastry recipe. Filled with a luxurious beer chocolate cream made with Costa Rica 38% milk chocolate and a touch of coffee, this dessert is a sensational treat for your senses.

COMPONENTS

For 30 choux of 80 g
Cocoa crumble
Cocoa choux pastry
Chocolate beer custard

CHOCOLATE AND BEER PAIRING

La Trappe Dubbel's rich caramel, dark fruit, and subtle spice notes enhance the flavor of the creamy custard made with Costa Rica 38% milk chocolate, which has smooth milk and vanilla flavors that make a delightful filling for choux pastries.

INGREDIENTS

Cocoa crumble
15 g/choux

butter	150 g
sugar	200 g
pastry flour	135 g
almond powder	30 g
Premium Dutch Cocoa Powder	20 g
salt	1 g

Cocoa choux pastry
30 g/choux

pastry flour	250 g
Premium Dutch Cocoa Powder	50 g
semi-skimmed milk	300 g
water	200 g
sugar	15 g
salt	3 g
butter	200 g
eggs	500 g

PREPARATION

Cocoa crumble
Mix the cold butter and the sugar in a stand mixer fitted with the paddle attachment.
Sift all the dry ingredients together.
Add these ingredients and continue mixing at low speed to obtain a homogeneous dough.
Put the dough in the fridge for a couple of hours.
Roll out the dough at 2 mm thick and cut out round discs 5 cm in diameter using a dough cutter.
Put these crumble dough discs on a tray in a fridge or freezer.
Place these on top of the choux pastries before baking.

Cocoa choux pastry
Sift the flour and the cocoa powder together.
Bring the milk, water, sugar, salt and butter to a boil.
Remove from the heat and add the sifted ingredients.
Mix with a spatula into a homogenous dough.
Return the dough to low heat and mix for 2 minutes using a spatula.
Pour this mixture into a stand mixer and mix for 1 minute with the paddle attachment at medium speed.
Add the eggs gradually and check the dough texture at the end.
Pipe choux circles, 5 cm in diameter onto a greased baking tray and put a cocoa crumble disc on top of each. Press down a bit so the choux dough is evenly distributed below the cocoa crumble.
Bake at 170 °C in a convection oven for about 10 minutes with dampers closed and 20 minutes with dampers open (exact timing will depend on your oven).
After baking, set aside to cool.

Chocolate beer custard
35 g/choux

milk	300 g
La Trappe Dubbel	300 g
soluble coffee	4 g
sugar	100 g
egg yolks	80 g
flour	30 g
corn starch	45 g
Costa Rica 38% milk chocolate	190 g
butter	60 g

Chocolate beer custard
Bring the milk, beer and soluble coffee to a boil with half of the sugar.
In a separate bowl, mix the other half of the sugar, the egg yolks, the corn starch and the flour with a whisk until homogenous.
Pour some of the boiling mixture onto the egg yolk mixture while whisking.
Then pour the lukewarm egg yolk mixture into the rest of the boiling mixture and return to the heat.
Bring to a boil, whisking constantly.
Boil for one minute while still whisking and then remove from the heat.
Add the chocolate and the butter.
Whisk until you have a homogeneous custard.
Pour the beer chocolate custard on a tray and cover with cling film.
Leave the tray with the custard to cool down on the table and then refrigerate.
When ready to assemble, stir the cream a bit in a bowl with a spatula and then fill the choux pastries.
Store them in the fridge at 4 °C.
For more on the chocolate decoration technique, please see p. 54.

Upcycled anise ganache cookie

Indulge yourself with this beer draff, Papua New Guinea 36% white chocolate, and anise cookie. Bitter beer draff, creamy white chocolate and aromatic anise blend perfectly for a unique, captivating flavor experience. Perfect with a fresh Kwak Blonde.

COMPONENTS

For 30 cookies of 35 g
Cookie with beer draff
Pipeable anise ganache
Chocolate decoration

CHOCOLATE AND BEER PAIRING

Kwak Blonde's delicate bitterness, fruity banana, and pear notes enhance the creamy anise and cooked milk flavors of Papua New Guinea 36% white ganache, making for a delightful combination with a crunchy beer draff cookie.

INGREDIENTS

Cookie with beer draff
20 g/cookie

butter	135 g
sugar	130 g
egg yolk	20 g
almond powder	90 g
beer draff	60 g
flour	190 g
baking soda	1 g
salt	2 g
Pure Prime Pressed Cocoa Butter	50 g

Pipeable anise ganache
10 g/cookie

cream (35% fat)	110 g
glucose	20 g
invert sugar	20 g
sorbitol	10 g
anise powder	1 g
Papua New Guinea 36% white chocolate	190 g
butter	35 g

Chocolate decoration
5 g/cookie

Papua New Guinea 36% white chocolate	250 g

PREPARATION

Cookie with beer draff

Mix the cold butter and the sugar in a stand mixer with the paddle attachment.
Sift all the dry ingredients together. Add the dry ingredients and the egg yolk.
Continue mixing at low speed to obtain a homogeneous dough.
Put the dough in the fridge for a couple of hours.
Roll the dough out at 4 mm thick and cut out cookies 5 cm in diameter.
Put the cookies on a Silpain® to avoid air bubbles during baking.
Bake at 165 °C for 20 minutes with dampers open, depending on the oven.
Leave to cool down.
Melt the cocoa butter and brush a thin layer on the side of the cookies where you will pipe the ganache.

Pipeable anise ganache

Heat the cream, glucose, invert sugar, sorbitol and anise powder until 80 °C.
Pour this over the Papua New Guinea 36% white chocolate and mix with a spatula to obtain a ganache.
When the ganache reaches a temperature of 35 °C, add the cold butter and mix for 2 minutes with an immersion blender.
Avoid incorporating air bubbles.
Pour the ganache on a tray and cover with cling film.
Leave to set at room temperature.

Chocolate decoration

Heat the Papua New Guinea 36% white chocolate to approximately 45 °C and temper on a marble slab to 28.5 °C.
Pipe dots 3 cm in diameter on a sheet of baking paper and immediately press a frozen silicone stamp onto the dots to create the swirl design.
Leave to crystallize for 1 hour.
Pipe some anise ganache on top of each cookie and place a white chocolate decoration on top.
Leave to set a bit and then store in a closed container in a cool place at around 18 °C.

For more on the decoration technique, see p. 64.

Beer cake and chocolate

This soft beer cake is a unique blend of flavors, coated with creamy Cameroon 45% milk chocolate and infused with the zesty notes of orange and rich Dobbel Palm beer. A delightful twist on a traditional dessert.

COMPONENTS

For 5 beer cakes of 350 g
Beer cake
Chocolate coating
Chocolate decoration

CHOCOLATE AND BEER PAIRING

Dobbel Palm's pronounced maltiness, caramel notes, and hints of toasted bread complements the rich, roasted cocoa, cooked milk, and caramel flavors of Cameroon 45% milk chocolate, creating a balanced coating for the beer cake.

INGREDIENTS

Beer cake
320 g/cake

butter	150 g
grapeseed oil	120 g
eggs	180 g
egg yolks	60 g
sugar	320 g
hopped malt powder (optional)	15 g
flour	410 g
milk powder	40 g
baking powder	5 g
salt	2 g
orange zest	10 g
Dobbel Palm	330 g

Chocolate coating
60 g/cake

Cameroon 45% milk chocolate	500 g
oil (room temperature)	50 g

Chocolate decoration
35 g/cake

Cameroon 45% milk chocolate	200 g

PREPARATION

Beer cake
Heat the oil and butter together to 35 °C.
Whip the eggs, egg yolks and sugar.
Sift all the dry ingredients together.
Mix in the fluffy egg mixture and the oil-butter mixture with a spatula.
Incorporate the beer and the orange zest, then add all other sifted ingredients.
Mix everything with a spatula until you have a homogeneous cake batter.
Use a rectangular cake mold 6 cm wide, 25 cm long and 6 cm high.
Butter the cake mold and dust with flour.
Pipe 320 g of beer cake batter into the mold.
Bake the cake at 175 °C for 10 minutes and lower the temperature to 165 °C.
Bake for another 15 minutes, depending on the oven, with dampers closed.
Remove the cake from the oven and unmold after 5 minutes.
Set aside to cool.
When the cake has cooled to around 40 °C, cover with cling film and let cool further for the next step.

Chocolate coating
Heat the Cameroon 45% milk chocolate to 45 °C and temper it to 30 °C on a marble slab.
Add the oil and mix with a spatula.
Cover the cake with this chocolate coating.
Leave the finished cake to crystallize before serving.

Chocolate decoration
Heat the Cameroon 45% milk chocolate to 45 °C and temper it to 29 °C on a marble slab.
Spread chocolate very thinly on the marble slab using an English pallet knife.
Wait for the right moment, when the chocolate is set and still flexible.
Scrape the chocolate from the table with a metal scraper to create a waved shape.
Put this on top of the coated cake.

Brussels chocolate beer waffle

Indulge in the ultimate Brussels waffle, crafted with beer for a light, airy texture and drizzled with a rich-tasting Papua New Guinea 70% dark chocolate.

COMPONENTS

For approximately 10 waffles of 110 g
Brussels beer waffle
Chocolate coating

CHOCOLATE AND BEER PAIRING

Delirium Tremens' fruity, spicy notes infuse the Brussels waffle, enhancing its flavor. The complex Papua New Guinea 70% dark chocolate on top adds richness, creating a balanced and delightful taste experience.

INGREDIENTS

Brussels beer waffle
110 g/waffle

eggs	3
milk	300 g
sugar	5 g
fresh yeast	20 g
strong bread flour	440 g
Delirium Tremens	300 g
salt	40 g
butter	200 g

Chocolate coating
15 g/waffle

Papua New Guinea 70% dark chocolate	250 g
icing sugar	as needed

PREPARATION

Brussels beer waffle

Separate the egg whites from the egg yolks.
Heat the milk to 30 °C and add the sugar and yeast; whisk briefly.
Add the flour and the egg yolks and whisk again.
Finally, add the beer and salt and whisk again.
Bring the butter to a boil until most of the water is evaporated and it takes on a nice golden color.
Add this to the waffle mixture and whisk very well.
In the meantime, whip the egg whites until fluffy.
Add the whipped egg white and fold gently into the waffle batter.
Dough temperature should be 28 °C.
Cover the bowl with a wet towel and leave to ferment for an hour at room temperature.
Use a pro-quality waffle iron and cook the waffles at approximately 220 °C for about 3.5 minutes.
Decorate (see below) and serve immediately.

Chocolate coating

Heat the Papua New Guinea 70% dark chocolate to approximately 48 °C and temper on a marble slab to 30 °C.
Spread out tempered chocolate between two guitar sheets and leave to set a bit.
Cut into rectangles the size of the waffles and leave to crystallize for 1 hour.
Unmold the thin chocolate rectangles and set aside.

When each waffle is freshly baked, put the waffle on a pre-heated serving plate and place a thin chocolate rectangle on top.
Dust with icing sugar.

Chocolate beer brownie

No chocolate recipe book would be complete without a brownie recipe, but this one contains beer. On top I've added some pecan pieces, and at the final stage, the brownie is decorated with a chocolate millefeuille flavored with Kerel Stout.

SWEET RETREAT

COMPONENTS

For 25 brownies of 80 g
Beer brownie
Pipeable beer ganache
Chocolate decoration

CHOCOLATE AND BEER PAIRING

Kerel Stout's deep roasted malt, coffee, and chocolate notes enhance the rich, woody, olive, and licorice flavors of Costa Rica 64% dark chocolate, creating a balanced, bittersweet brownie.

INGREDIENTS

Beer brownie
80 g/brownie

butter	330 g
Costa Rica 64% dark chocolate	225 g
eggs	300 g
sugar	510 g
Premium Dutch Cocoa Powder	80 g
pastry flour	260 g
Kerel Stout (room temperature)	450 g
salt	3 g
pecan pieces	300 g

Pipeable beer ganache
20 g/brownie

Kerel Stout	100 g
cream (35% fat)	100 g
glucose	50 g
invert sugar	30 g
Costa Rica 64% dark chocolate	200 g
butter	30 g

Chocolate decoration
10 g/brownie

Costa Rica 64% dark chocolate	300 g

PREPARATION

Beer brownie

Heat the butter with the Costa Rica 64% dark chocolate to 45 °C.
Whisk the eggs and the sugar until light and aerated.
Sift the cocoa powder and the flour together.
Fold the chocolate mixture into the aerated egg composition with a spatula.
Add the sifted ingredients and mix with the spatula.
Add the stout and the salt and mix until you have a homogeneous brownie batter.
Pour into a 30 x 40 cm tray and sprinkle with broken pecans.
Bake at 170 °C for 30 minutes with dampers closed and 5 minutes at 165 °C with dampers open (exact timing will depend on your oven).
Leave to cool and cut out circles in the appropriate size.

Pipeable beer ganache

Heat the beer, cream, glucose and invert sugar to 80 °C.
Pour over the Costa Rica 64% dark chocolate and mix with a spatula to create an emulsion.
When the ganache reaches a temperature of 35 °C, add the cold butter and mix for 2 minutes with an immersion blender.
Pour the beer ganache on a tray, cover with cling film and leave to cool to room temperature.
Decorate the brownie by piping some ganache on top and placing a chocolate decoration on the ganache.
Repeat this a couple of times on the same brownie.

Chocolate decoration

Heat the Costa Rica 64% dark chocolate to approximately 48 °C and temper on a marble slab to 30 °C.
Spread out the chocolate very thin between two guitar sheets.
Cut out circles of different sizes using dough cutters.
Leave to crystallize for 1 hour before removing the guitar sheets.
For making the decoration, see p. 57.

Amber blondie beer caramel

A soft blonde brownie topped with almond cubes. This recipe also features a delicious salted beer caramel. There could hardly be a more indulgent application of Selection Amber 30% chocolate.

SWEET RETREAT

COMPONENTS

For a frame of 30 x 40 cm
Amber blondie
Salted beer caramel
Amber nutty coating

CHOCOLATE AND BEER PAIRING

The caramel brownie made with Selection Amber chocolate offers a rich, buttery, and smooth caramel flavor. The soft caramel filling, infused with Bolleke De Koninck beer, adds a malty sweetness that perfectly complements the chocolate.

INGREDIENTS

Amber blondie
20 g/portion

butter	300 g
Selection Amber 30% chocolate	480 g
whole eggs	360 g
sugar	320 g
brown sugar	60 g
invert sugar	70 g
flour	250 g
baking powder	2 g
sea salt	3 g
egg white	120 g
almond cubes	100 g

Salted beer caramel
60 g/portion

Bolleke De Koninck (to soak the gelatin)	90 g
gelatin powder	15 g
glucose	150 g
sugar	360 g
cream (35% fat)	500 g
Bolleke De Konink	200 g
butter	250 g
sea salt	4 g
Selection Amber 30% chocolate	150 g

Amber nutty coating
20 g/portion

Selection Amber 30% chocolate	500 g
oil	50 g
roasted almond cubes	150 g

PREPARATION

Amber blondie
Heat the butter with the Selection Amber 30% chocolate to 40 °C. Don't overmix.
Whip the whole eggs with the sugar, brown sugar and invert sugar.
Combine with the chocolate and use a spatula to incorporate the sifted flour, baking powder and sea salt.
Whip the egg whites until stiff then fold them in with a spatula.
Pour into a baking frame (5 cm high) on a 30 x 40 cm baking tray.
Decorate with the almond cubes and bake at 170 °C for 30 minutes (depending on the oven) with dampers closed.
Let cool in the frame and freeze.

Salted beer caramel
Bring the beer (90 g) to a gentle boil and set aside to cool.
Once the beer is cooled, soak the gelatin in it.
Put the glucose in a pan and then add the sugar.
Boil the glucose and sugar until you have a nicely colored caramel.
Meanwhile, heat the cream, the beer and the butter to 80 °C.
Add gradually to the caramel, whisking constantly.
Heat this mixture to 103 °C.
Now add the sea salt and the soaked gelatin.
Leave the mixture to cool down until it reaches 40 °C.
Add the Selection Amber 30% chocolate and mix with an immersion blender.
Finally, pour the caramel on top of the blondie.
Leave to set overnight in the freezer and cut into the desired shapes.

Amber nutty coating
Heat the Selection Amber 30% chocolate to 38 °C .
Add the oil and the chopped roasted almond cubes.
Dip the frozen blondies in the coating at approximately 30 °C.
Leave to set on a sheet of baking paper.

Beer Bonbon Boutique

Bouchée René Coriander praliné

Experience an unforgettable taste journey of a beer-fruit paste and a citrusy, nutty coriander praliné. Covered with a pure bittersweet exotic fruit tasting Philippines 68% dark chocolate.

COMPONENTS

For 60 bouchées of 23 g
Fruit paste cherry Cuveé René
Coriander almond praliné
Enrobing

CHOCOLATE AND BEER PAIRING

This recipe creates a perfect marriage by combining the tropical fruit notes of Philippines 68% dark chocolate with the sour, lemony flavors of Cuvée René beer. Cherry fruit in the bonbon balances the flavors beautifully.

INGREDIENTS

Fruit paste cherry Cuveé René
8 g/portion

citric acid crystals	3 g
water	3 g
Lindemans Old Geuze Cuveé René	270 g
cherry puree	90 g
sugar	325 g
pectin yellow	14 g
sugar	40 g
invert sugar	70 g

Coriander almond praliné
10 g/portion

almonds (peeled)	140 g
hazelnuts (peeled)	140 g
sugar	120 g
coriander seeds	20 g
Selection Milk 35% chocolate	160 g
Pure Prime Pressed Cocoa Butter	25 g
ghee (concentrated butter)	30 g

Enrobing
5 g/portion

Philippines 68% dark chocolate	300 g
cocoa nibs	30 g

PREPARATION

Fruit paste cherry Cuveé René
Heat the citric acid crystals and the water in a small cup in the microwave.
Heat the cherry puree, the Old Geuze Cuveé René beer and the sugar (325 g) to 50 °C.
Dry mix the pectin with the sugar (40 g) and add it to the cherry-beer mixture.
Bring to a boil, whisking constantly.
When this boils, add the invert sugar and boil to 107 °C.
Remove the pan from the heat, add the citric solution and whisk.
Using a dosing funnel, pour immediately into silicone bouchée molds.
Fill the molds halfway and leave the beer fruit paste to cool.

TIP ⟶ *Boiling to only 103 °C without the citric acid will give you a pipeable jelly for molded chocolate applications.*

Coriander almond praliné
Roast the almonds and the hazelnuts and set aside to cool on a silicone sheet.
Melt the sugar in a pan and, when caramelized, add the coriander seeds.
Leave everything to cool completely. Pour this over the roasted nuts and leave to cool.
Once cooled, put the nut caramel mixture in a robot cutter and mix to obtain a thick, semi-liquid paste.
Melt the chocolate and the cocoa butter to 45 °C and add the ghee.
Add this to the praliné and temper the filling to 26 °C on a marble slab.
Pipe the filling onto the fruit paste cherry Cuveé René and place in a fridge of 5 °C for about 5 minutes.
Once crystallized, unmold them from the silicone mold and keep them at hand for the next step.

Enrobing
Heat the Philippines 68% dark chocolate to approximately 47 °C.
Temper the chocolate at 29.4 °C on a marble slab.
Dip and enrobe the bouchées for the first time and sprinkle with some cocoa nibs.
Once the chocolate is dry, enrobe them a second time.

TIP ⟶ *For an extra touch of creativity, you can add some tempered white chocolate over the second layer of dark chocolate when enrobing (as in the picture of the Bouchée René).*

Guinness mallow hops ganache

Single Origins Chocolate ganache infused with Fuggles hops, perfectly complemented by a fluffy Guinness beer marshmallow. A harmonious blend of rich flavors, this unique dessert will tantalize your taste buds and elevate your culinary experience.

COMPONENTS

For 200 bonbons of 11 g
Molding
Hops ganache
Guinness mallow
Chocolate dip

CHOCOLATE AND BEER PAIRING

Combine the woody, coffee notes of Costa Rica 64% dark chocolate with the malty sweetness and roasted flavors of Guinness. A ganache infused with Fuggles hops adds earthy undertones, while Guinness Extra Stout beer marshmallow provides a fluffy touch of sweetness.

INGREDIENTS

Molding
2 g/bonbon

Selection Dark Intense 65% chocolate	500 g

Hops ganache
4 g/bonbon

Fuggles hop pellets	1 g
water	25 g
cream 35% fat	320 g
glucose	35 g
sorbitol	15 g
Costa Rica 64% dark chocolate	300 g
Costa Rica 38% milk chocolate	75 g
butter	40 g

Guinness mallow
3 g/bonbon

Guinness Extra Stout (to soak the gelatin)	105 g
gelatin powder	18 g
Guinness Extra Stout	200 g
sugar	170 g
invert sugar	150 g

PREPARATION

Molding
Heat the chocolate to 47 °C and temper to 29.4 °C on a marble slab.
Mold the polycarbonate bonbon molds with the tempered chocolate.
Leave to set at 16 °C for 1 hour with a relative humidity level below 60% before you fill them.
Mold: Chocolate World CW1575

Hops ganache
Soak the hop pellets in the cold water for 30 minutes.
Add to the cream, and then add the glucose and sorbitol.
Heat this to approximately 85 °C.
Strain this hot mixture through a sieve over the chocolates.
Mix with a spatula to obtain a ganache.
When the ganache reaches a temperature of 35 °C, add the cold butter and mix with an immersion blender.
Use the ganache at a maximum temperature of 30 °C.
Pipe the ganache into the chocolate molds and keep 2 mm from the edge of the mold.
Leave some space to pipe the Guinness mallow on top.
Leave to crystallize for 2 hours in a cool, dry place before you start the mallow preparation.

Guinness mallow
Give the Guinness (105 g) a short boil and leave to cool.
When this beer is cooled, add the gelatin powder and leave to soak for 10 minutes.
Bring the Guinness (200 g), sugar and invert sugar to a boil for 2 minutes at medium heat.
Remove from the heat.
Put the gelatine beer mass in a stand mixer fitted with the whisk attachment.
Add the warm sugar beer syrup at 90 °C on top of the gelatin beer mass and start to whisk.
When the fluffy beer mallow mass reaches 30 °C, you can pipe it on top of the hops ganache.
Immediately insert a small bamboo skewer (see picture) and leave to set and crystalize for 12 hours in a cool, dry place.

Chocolate dip
2 g/bonbon

Selection Dark Intense 65% chocolate	500 g

Chocolate dip

Heat the chocolate to 47 °C and temper to 29.4 °C on a marble slab.
Take the crystallized mallow bonbons out of the mold, one by one, by pulling gently on the bamboo skewer.
Dip the bonbons in the tempered chocolate to cover the mallow halfway.
Place the dipped bonbons on a sheet of baking paper and leave to crystallize for 30 minutes in a cool, dry place.
Store them in a cool, dry place at 16 °C and with a relative humidity level below 60%.

TIP ⟶ *You can freeze leftover mallow in an oiled container, then cut into pieces and dust with humidity-resistant icing sugar or deco-sugar for a delicious bite-sized snack!*

Ultimate beer bottle bonbon

Revel in the rich, decadent flavor of the ultimate beer ganache bonbon. This unique confection blends the bold essence of beer with silky-smooth chocolate ganache for an unforgettable gourmet experience.

COMPONENTS

For 120 bonbons of 11 g
Molding
Beer syrup for ganache
Ultimate beer ganache

CHOCOLATE AND BEER PAIRING

The deep roasted cocoa and caramel notes of Cameroon 45% milk chocolate contrast with the rich, malty sweetness and fruity esters of Westmalle Trappist Dubbel. Cascade hops add a hint of floral bitterness to the ganache.

INGREDIENTS

Molding
4 g/bonbon

Cameroon 45% milk chocolate	as needed
gold powder	as needed

Beer syrup for ganache

coriander seeds	3 g
orange peel	5 g
Westmalle Trappist Dubbel	250 g
glucose	50 g
sugar	20 g
Cascade hop pellets	1 g

Ultimate beer ganache
7 g/bonbon

beer syrup	230 g
sorbitol powder	20 g
Cameroon 45% milk chocolate	440 g
Selection Dark Intense 65% chocolate	80 g
cream (35% fat)	50 g
butter (82% fat)	80 g

PREPARATION

Molding
Spray some gold powder in the mold with a small gold pump.
Heat the Cameroon 45% milk chocolate to 47 °C and temper to 29 °C on a marble slab.
Mold the colored polycarbonate bonbon molds. Before filling, leave to set for 1 hour at 16 °C with a relative humidity level below 60%.
Mold: Chocolate World CW2037

Beer syrup for ganache
Roast the coriander seeds lightly in a pan and set aside to cool.
Crush the coriander seeds with a mortar and pestle.
Wash the oranges and cut off some large slices of peel without too much white pith.
Boil the beer with the glucose, sugar, hop pellets, coriander seeds and orange peel.
Cover the boiling pan with cling film and leave to infuse for 10 minutes.
Strain out the orange peel and the coriander and reserve the beer syrup for the next step.

Ultimate beer ganache
Bring the beer syrup and the sorbitol powder to a boil.
Pour over the Cameroon 45% milk chocolate and the Selection Dark Intense 65% chocolate.
Mix with a spatula to obtain a ganache texture.
Heat the cream in the same pan to approximately 50 °C and pour over the ganache.
Continue mixing with a spatula to obtain a ganache with a temperature between 35 and 38 °C.
Mix with an immersion blender to create a perfect emulsion.
Add the cold butter and mix again with the immersion blender.
Use the ganache immediately at a temperature of no more than 29 °C.
Fill the molds with the ultimate beer ganache and leave to crystallize for 12 hours overnight in a cool and dry place.
Finish the molds with tempered Cameroon 45% milk chocolate and unmold after crystallization.

Crystal beer syrup bonbon

If you've ever wanted to make a beer syrup praline instead of a liquor one, this is your chance. A crystal beer syrup bonbon made with a Saison Dupont beer and a bittersweet Philippines 68% dark chocolate, with a delightful flavor that entices you on a liquid taste adventure.

COMPONENTS

For 120 bonbons of 10 g
Molding
Beer syrup with alcohol
Closing of the mold

CHOCOLATE AND BEER PAIRING

The tropical fruit notes of Philippines 68% dark chocolate combine with Saison Dupont's lemony, peppery flavors in the form of a crystal beer syrup. This liquid syrup creates a pleasant, balanced flavor profile with some sweetness.

INGREDIENTS

Molding
2 g/bonbon

Philippines 68% dark chocolate	500 g

Beer syrup with alcohol
7 g/bonbon

Saison Dupont beer	300 g
sugar	500 g
glucose	20 g
pure alcohol 96%	100 g

Closing of the mold
1 g/bonbon

Philippines 68% dark chocolate	250 g

PREPARATION

Molding
Heat the chocolate to 47 °C and temper to 29.4 °C on a marble slab.
Mold the colored chocolate bonbon polycarbonate bonbon molds.
Leave to set for 1 hour at 16 °C with a relative humidity level below 60% before you fill them.
Mold: Chocolate World CW1521

Beer syrup with alcohol
Boil the beer, sugar and glucose at 106 °C.
During the boiling process, brush the sides of the pan with clean water to clean them.
Remove the foam from the cooking syrup with a small sieve.
Once the correct temperature has been reached, cool the syrup down by pouring it back and forth between two stainless steel bowls.
Repeat this movement until the syrup has cooled down to 70 °C.
Never use a whisk or spatula to stir the syrup.
Add the pure alcohol and repeat the movement from one bowl to the other until the syrup has cooled down to 30 °C (but do not allow to go below 20 °C).
Pipe the syrup into the chocolate molds and leave to crystallize at room temperature for about 30 hours.
After filling, don't move the molds until the sugar syrup has crystallized.

Closing the mold
After 30 hours of crystallization of the beer syrup, close the molds gently with tempered chocolate and unmold after crystallization.
Store the bonbons in a cool and dry place.

Cherry beer chocolate ganache

I like Lindemans Kriek beer a lot, so I couldn't resist making a cherry beer bonbon in combination with the Vietnam 73% dark chocolate. A delightful balance of flavors that promises a fruity-tart beer chocolate taste adventure.

COMPONENTS

For 120 bonbons of 11 g
Molding
Cherry beer ganache
Chocolate decoration

CHOCOLATE AND BEER PAIRING

Complementing the pronounced acidic and citrusy notes of Vietnam 73% dark chocolate with the sour cherry flavors of Lindemans Kriek beer, creating a chocolate ganache that balances fruity acidity with rich, dark chocolate complexity.

INGREDIENTS

Molding
3 g/bonbon

Selection Dark Intense 65% chocolate	as needed

Cherry beer ganache
6 g/bonbon

Lindemans Kriek	125 g
cherry puree	20 g
glucose	40 g
sorbitol	15 g
Citric acid crystals	2 g
Vietnam 73% dark chocolate	110 g
Selection White Intense 31% chocolate	225 g
butter (82% fat)	35 g

Chocolate decoration
1 g/bonbon

Selection Milk 35% chocolate	100 g

PREPARATION

Molding
Color the mold with tempered red-colored cocoa butter (see p. 50).
Immediately swirl with a cotton swab in the mold and dust with some silver powder for a pearly effect.
Heat the chocolate to 47 °C and temper to 29.4 °C on a marble slab.
Mold the colored polycarbonate bonbon molds. Let set for 1 hour at 16 °C with a relative humidity level below 60% before you fill them.
Mold: Chocolate World CW1867

Cherry beer ganache
Boil the cherry beer, cherry puree, glucose, sorbitol and citric acid crystals.
Pour over the chocolates and mix with a spatula to obtain an emulsion.
When the ganache reaches a temperature of 35 °C, add the cold butter and mix with an immersion blender.
Use the ganache at 29 °C.
Pipe the ganache into the chocolate molds and leave to crystallize for 12 hours at 16 °C and a relative humidity below 60%.
Close the molds with tempered chocolate and unmold after full crystallization.

Chocolate decoration
Heat the chocolate to 45 °C and temper to 29 °C on a marble slab.
Pipe a small drop of approximately 1 g onto a sheet of baking paper and push it down with a frozen silicone stamp (see p. 64).
Leave the decoration to crystalize for about 30 minutes.
Remove the decoration from the paper and glue it on top of a cherry beer bonbon by piping some tempered chocolate onto the bonbon and gently pressing a chocolate decoration onto it.
Store the bonbons in a cool and dry place.

TIP ⟶ *You can also extend the shelf life of this ganache by adding 1% of pure alcohol on the total weight of the ganache.*

Amber full beer caramel

Savor the luxurious blend of beer-flavored caramel and caramelized chocolate pralines, featuring a gooey filling that melts in your mouth. Perfect for a sophisticated treat or to impress your guests!

COMPONENTS

For approximately 80 bonbons of 11 g
Molding
Beer Caramel

CHOCOLATE AND BEER PAIRING

Complementing the balanced salted butter caramel notes of Selection Amber chocolate with the fruity, spicy flavors of Orvélo Tripel beer, creating a beer caramel with chocolate that unites sweet and malty richness.

INGREDIENTS

Molding
4 g/bonbon

Selection Amber 30% chocolate	as needed

Beer caramel
7 g/bonbon

cream 35% fat	200 g
sugar	135 g
glucose	50 g
Orvélo Tripel Beer	200 g
Selection Amber 30% chocolate	50 g
Pure Prime Pressed Cocoa Butter	10 g
butter	50 g

PREPARATION

Molding
Melt the Selection Amber 30% chocolate to 45 °C and temper it at 28 °C on a marble slab.
Mold the colored polycarbonate bonbon molds with tempered chocolate and leave to crystalize for 1 hour.
For coloring the molds, see basic techniques: "coloring of chocolate molds" p. 50.
Mold: Chocolate World CW2116

Beer caramel
Heat the cream and make a blond caramel with the sugar and the glucose in another bowl.
Deglaze the blond caramel with the warm cream and cook this mixture to 110 °C.
Add the beer and cook it again to 105 °C.
Add the Selection Amber 30% chocolate and the cocoa butter and mix with an immersion blender.
When the caramel reaches 35 °C, add the cold butter and mix again with an immersion blender for 2 minutes.
When the caramel has a temperature of 28 °C, pipe it in the chocolate shells and leave to crystallize for 24 hours at 16 °C with a relative humidity below 60%.
After crystallization, close the bonbons with tempered Selection Amber 30% chocolate and leave to crystalize for 30 minutes before unmolding.
Store them in a cool dry place.

Chocolate beer orangettes

Experience a traditional orangette but boiled in a beer syrup. This gives the candied oranges an extra bitterness with a light fermented flavor. The enrobing with the Philippines 68% dark chocolate caps off the rich, exotic and fruity taste experience.

COMPONENTS

For approximately 2kg of beer orangettes
Beer orangettes confit
Enrobing & finishing

CHOCOLATE AND BEER PAIRING

The orange peels bathed in a La Trappe Tripel beer syrup, with fruity peach and apricot notes complement with the Philippines 68% dark chocolate, featuring tropical fruits, red berries, and a hint of pepper.

INGREDIENTS

Beer orangettes confit
6 g/portion

orange peels	1000 g
water	2 l
sugar	1200 g
water	450 g
La Trappe Tripel	750 g
glucose	75 g
sugar (day 2)	300 g
sugar (day 3)	300 g

Enrobing & finishing
4 g/portion

Dextrose	100 g
Premium Dutch Cocoa Powder	100 g
Philippines 68% dark chocolate	1000 g

TIP ⟶ *You can also use grapefruit or pomelo fruit peels for this application, which will give an extra tangy flavor that pairs well with IPA beers.*

PREPARATION

Beer orangettes confit
Wash 5 kg of oranges and peel them.
Cut the peel into long strips 1 cm thick.
Boil 2 l of water and add the orange peels; leave to simmer for 10 minutes.
Remove the orange peels from the boiling water and rinse them with cold water.
Make a sugar syrup by boiling the 1200 g of sugar, 450 g water, the beer and the glucose.
Skim off the foam with a sieve when it starts to boil.
Add the orange peels and bring to a simmering boil for 5 minutes.
Leave the orange peels to cool in the syrup overnight.
Strain to separate the orange peels from the beer sugar syrup, reserving the syrup.
Add 300 g of sugar (day 2) to the beer sugar syrup and bring to a boil.
Add the orange peels and simmer for 5 minutes.
Leave to cool overnight.
Repeat this method again with the sugar (day 3).
On the fourth day you can remove the candied orange peels from the syrup using a strainer.
Leave the candied orange peels to drip out overnight.

Enrobing and finishing
Dust the orange peel with the dextrose and shake them in a sieve to remove the excess dextrose.
Add the cocoa powder and gently mix a bit by hand.
Put the orange peel in a sieve and shake off the excess cocoa powder.
Heat the Philippines 68% dark chocolate to approximately 48 °C and temper on a marble slab to 30 °C.
Dip the pieces of candied beer orange peel in the chocolate one by one using a dipping fork and place them on a sheet of baking paper.
Leave to crystallize in a cool, dry place of about 16 °C.
Store in a cool, dry place with a relative humidity level below 60%.

Bonbon Beer Pairings

Pesto salty lemon

This bonbon is inspired by two items I like very much: Italian pesto and the salty lemons from Morocco used in tajines. This combination is well-balanced by the sweetness of the Selection White Intense 31% chocolate.

COMPONENTS

For 100 bonbons of 9.5 g
Molding
Salty Lemon Confit
Pesto ganache

CHOCOLATE AND BEER PAIRING

White Hoegaarden beer, with its refreshing citrus and coriander notes, prepares the palate beautifully for tasting the creamy sweetness of white chocolate pesto ganache and the tangy zest of salty lemon jelly.

INGREDIENTS

Molding
3 g/bonbon

Selection White Intense 31% chocolate	as needed

Salty lemon confit
2.5 g/bonbon

lemon zest	30 g
lemon juice (freshly squeezed)	75 g
water	50 g
maltodextrin (or sugar)	50 g
glucose	200 g
citric acid	0.5 g
Himalayan salt	2 g

Pesto ganache
4 g/bonbon

cream (35% fat)	125 g
glucose	15 g
sorbitol crystals	15 g
invert sugar	12 g
Selection White Intense 31% chocolate	250 g
Pure Prime Pressed Cocoa Butter	12 g
butter	20 g
pesto (home-made or jarred)	50 g

PREPARATION

Molding
Heat the Selection White Intense 31% chocolate to 45 °C and temper it to 28 °C on a marble slab.
Mold the pre-colored polycarbonate molds with the tempered chocolate and leave to crystallize for 1 hour.
For coloring the molds, see basic techniques: "coloring of chocolate molds" p. 50.
Mold: Chocolate World CW1867

Salty lemon confit
Wash the lemons (3) and zest them with a microplane.
Juice the lemons.
Combine all the ingredients and boil at 104 °C.
Transfer to a bowl and cover with cling film.
Leave to cool to room temperature.
Fill the chocolate shell with the confit to 1/3.
If using sugar instead of maltodextrin, the confit will be slightly sweeter.

Pesto ganache
Boil the fresh cream with the glucose and the sorbitol crystals and add the invert sugar.
Pour over the Selection White Intense 31% chocolate and the cocoa butter.
Mix the preparation with an immersion blender into a homogeneous and smooth filling.
When the ganache reaches 35 °C, add the cold butter and the pesto and keep blending until just incorporated.
Let the ganache cool until it reaches a temperature of 28 °C.
Pipe the pesto ganache into the mold on top of the salty lemon confit.
Leave to crystallize for 12 hours at 16 °C with a relative humidity below 60%.
Close with tempered chocolate and a custom-designed transfer sheet, see p. 51, and unmold after setting.
Store in a cool, dry place.

Tomato lemon pistachio

The tangy-sweet tomato jelly, creamy white chocolate pistachio ganache and refreshing lemon zest create a unique, impressive bonbon. Rub the calyx between your fingers before placing the bonbon in your mouth.

COMPONENTS

For 120 bonbons of 12 g
Molding
Sweet cherry tomato confit
Lemon pistachio ganache

CHOCOLATE AND BEER PAIRING

Kwaremont beer, with its malty sweetness and subtle bitterness, cleanses the mouth between tastes of creamy richness and nutty flavor of white chocolate pistachio ganache with its nutty flavor and the savory-sweet twist of tomato jelly.

INGREDIENTS

Molding
4 g/bonbon

Selection White Intense 31% chocolate	250 g
Selection Dark Intense 65% chocolate	250 g

Sweet cherry tomato confit
4 g/bonbon

lemon zest	5 g
cherry tomatoes (mixed colors)	400 g
sugar	40 g
pectin	10 g
concentrated tomato puree	50 g
glucose	40 g
white vinegar	5 g
sea salt	2 g

PREPARATION

Molding

This bonbon is molded on two sides or using a double mold.
Spray half of your molds with red colored cocoa butter and leave to crystallize (see p. 50).
Heat the Selection White Intense 31% chocolate to 45 °C and temper it on a marble slab at 28.5 °C.
Mold the prepared red molds with tempered chocolate and leave to crystallize for at least one hour before filling.
Heat the Selection Dark Intense 65% chocolate to 47 °C and temper it on a marble slab at 29.4 °C.
Mold the other half of your molds with this tempered chocolate and leave to crystallize for at least one hour before filling.
Mold: Chocolate World CW1847

Sweet cherry tomato confit

Wash the lemon and zest it finely using a microplane.
Wash the cherry tomatoes and cut them into 8 pieces each.
Heat and simmer the cherry tomatoes for a few minutes in a pan with a lid to keep the moisture in.
In the meantime, combine the pectin and sugar and add this mixture to the tomatoes while whisking.
Add the concentrated tomato puree, the glucose and the lemon zest and boil for a few minutes at medium heat.
Push the mixture through a sieve and then boil at 102.5 °C while continuously whisking.
Add the vinegar and the sea salt, cover with cling film and leave to cool.
Pipe the sweet tomato confit into both molds and leave space for the pistachio ganache (2 g/mold).

Lemon pistachio ganache
4 g/bonbon

lemon zest	3 g
pistachios	65 g
cream (35% fat)	115 g
glucose	35 g
sorbitol crystals	10 g
Selection White Intense 31% chocolate	190 g
Pure Prime Pressed Cocoa Butter	45 g
butter (82% fat)	35 g

Lemon pistachio ganache
Wash the lemon and zest it finely with a microplane.
Lightly roast the pistachios and set aside to cool.
Mix the pistachios into a thick liquid paste with a robot cutter.
Bring the cream, glucose, sorbitol crystals and lemon zest to a gentle boil briefly, then pour over the Selection White Intense 31% chocolate and the cocoa butter.
Using a spatula, mix into a ganache. Keep at a maximum temperature of 38 °C.
Add the pistachio paste and mix with an immersion blender.
When the ganache reaches a temperature of 35 °C, add the cold butter and mix again with the immersion blender.
Cool to below 28 °C and use the ganache immediately. Pipe the ganache on top of the sweet cherry tomato confit to fill each mold.
Immediately put the two molds together while the ganache is still soft; this will ensure they stay together after unmolding.
Use small metal rods in the holes of the molds to keep the molds perfectly centered.
Leave to crystallize overnight in a cool, dry place at 16 °C and a relative humidity level below 60%.

Amber soy sauce speculoos

Soy sauce's savory, umami depth mingles perfectly with the spiced, molasses notes of speculoos. Almond nut paste adds a creamy, nutty richness, while caramel chocolate brings a buttery sweetness. Together, these flavors create a fascinating fusion.

COMPONENTS

For approximately 100 bonbons of 9 g
Molding
Soy sauce Amber ganache
Speculoos almond praliné

CHOCOLATE AND BEER PAIRING

The spicy hops, citrus, and honey notes of Saison Dottignies contrast beautifully with Amber chocolate's salted butter caramel and vanilla. The umami richness of soy sauce caramel pairs well with speculoos cookies praliné and the roasted buckwheat.

INGREDIENTS

Molding
3 g/bonbon

Selection Amber 30% chocolate	as needed

Soy sauce Amber ganache
4 g/bonbon

cream (35% fat)	125 g
glucose	10 g
sorbitol crystals	10 g
Selection Amber 30% chocolate	260 g
Pure Prime Pressed Cocoa Butter	25 g
sweet soy sauce	50 g
butter	35 g

Speculoos almond praliné
3 g/bonbon

almonds, peeled	120 g
sugar	80 g
Selection Amber 30% chocolate	50 g
Pure Prime Pressed Cocoa Butter	15 g
roasted buckwheat (sobacho)	8 g
speculoos cookie crumbs	70 g

PREPARATION

Molding
Heat the Selection Amber 30% chocolate to 45 °C and temper it to 28 °C on a marble slab.
Mold the pre-colored molds with tempered chocolate and leave to crystallize for 1 hour.
For coloring the molds, see basic techniques: "coloring of chocolate molds" p. 50.
Mold: Chocolate World CW1217

Soy sauce Amber ganache
Heat the cream, glucose, and sorbitol crystals to 85 °C. Pour the mixture over the Selection Amber 30% chocolate and cocoa butter and mix with an immersion blender.
Add the sweet soy sauce and mix again.
When the ganache cools to 35 °C, add the cold butter and mix again.
When the ganache reaches a temperature of 28 °C, pipe it into the chocolate shells, filling them up to 2/3.
Leave to crystallize for two hours at 16 °C with a relative humidity below 60%.

Speculoos almond praliné
Roast the almonds lightly and leave them on a silicone sheet to cool.
Dry caramelize the sugar and pour over the almonds.
Set aside to cool.
Once cooled, mix with a robot cutter into a thick liquid paste and set aside.
Heat the chocolate and the cocoa butter to 45 °C and add the almond praliné.
Temper the filling to 26 °C on a marble slab.
Add the roasted buckwheat and speculoos cookie crumbs and mix with a spatula.
Pipe the speculoos almond praliné on top of the soy sauce Amber ganache and leave to set for about 5 minutes in a cold fridge.
Melt and temper some Selection Amber 30% chocolate to close the molds and leave to crystallize.
Unmold and store in a cool, dry place.

Goat cheese balsamic

A tangy combination of creamy goat cheese and balsamic vinegar creates an intriguing contrast. The addition of caramel chocolate introduces a rich, buttery sweetness, harmonizing the flavors.

COMPONENTS

For 100 bonbons of 12 g
Molding
Caramel balsamic
Goat cheese ganache

CHOCOLATE AND BEER PAIRING

The refreshing fruity and floral notes and a hint of bitterness from the Omer Blond, complement the creamy tang of goat cheese white chocolate ganache and the rich, sweet-vinegar flavor of balsamic caramel wonderfully.

INGREDIENTS

Molding
2 g/each bonbon

Selection Amber 30% chocolate	as needed
Selection Milk 35% chocolate	as needed

Caramel balsamic
2.5 g/bonbon

sugar	120 g
glucose	50 g
cream (35% fat)	120 g
butter	60 g
sea salt	2 g
Selection Amber 30% chocolate	50 g
balsamic vinegar (Di Modena DOP)	50 g

Goat cheese ganache
5.5 g/bonbon

cream (35% fat)	115 g
glucose	20 g
sorbitol crystals	15 g
invert sugar	20 g
Selection White Intense 31% chocolate	240 g
Pure Prime Pressed Cocoa Butter	20 g
goat cheese (Chavroux type)	80 g
butter	15 g

PREPARATION

Molding
Heat the Selection Amber 30% chocolate to 45 °C and temper it to 28.2 °C on a marble slab. Mold the bonbon molds and leave to crystallize.
Mold: Chocolate World CW1604
Heat the Selection Milk 35% chocolate to 45 °C and temper it to 29 °C on a marble slab. Mold the bonbon molds and leave to crystallize.
Mold: Chocolate World CW1603

Caramel balsamic
Make a caramel with the sugar and the glucose.
Heat the cream and the butter.
Add this to the caramel gradually, along with the sea salt.
Leave the caramel to cool to 35 °C and then add the Selection Amber 30% chocolate (drops, not melted).
Mix with an immersion blender to create an emulsion.
Add the balsamic vinegar and mix again.
Fill the top molds with the caramel balsamic and leave to set for 12 hours.
After, close gently with tempered Selection Amber 30% chocolate and unmold after a few minutes.

Goat cheese ganache
Boil the fresh cream together with the glucose and the sorbitol crystals.
Add the invert sugar and pour the mixture over the Selection White Intense 31% chocolate, the cocoa butter and the goat cheese.
Mix with an immersion blender. When the ganache has cooled to a temperature of 35 °C, add the cold butter and mix again.
Pipe the ganache into the bottom mold and leave to crystallize for 12 hours at 16 °C with a relative humidity below 60%.
Finish after crystallization with tempered Selection Milk 35% chocolate and unmold after a few minutes.

Horseradish beetroot

A forgotten ingredient brought back to life in this surprising combination of horseradish and sweet beetroot. A masterpiece of flavors, it pairs brilliantly with a semi-sweet Selection White Intense chocolat.

COMPONENTS

For 120 bonbons of 8 g
Molding
Beetroot strawberry jelly
Horseradish ganache

CHOCOLATE AND BEER PAIRING

Liefmans Goudenband's rich, fruity, and slightly sour notes cleanse the palate excellently after the earthy sweetness of beetroot jelly and the sharp, creamy flavor of horseradish white chocolate ganache.

INGREDIENTS

Molding
3 g/bonbon

Selection White Intense 31% chocolate	as needed

Beetroot strawberry jelly
2 g/bonbon

sugar	120 g
pectin NH	3 g
beetroot, steamed	150 g
strawberry puree	110 g
maltodextrin (or sugar)	25 g
glucose	45 g
citric acid crystals	0.5 g
vinegar	2 g

Horseradish ganache
3 g/bonbon

cream (35% fat)	100 g
maltodextrin	15 g
sorbitol crystals	15 g
glucose	30 g
Selection White Intense 31% chocolate	250 g
Pure Prime Pressed Cocoa Butter	15 g
horseradish cream paste (jarred)	50 g
butter	25 g

PREPARATION

Molding
Heat the Selection White Intense 31% chocolate to 45 °C and temper it to 28 °C on a marble slab.
Mold the pre-colored molds with the tempered chocolate and leave to crystallize for 1 hour.
For coloring the molds, see basic techniques: "coloring of chocolate molds" p. 50.
Mold: Chocolate World CW1903

Beetroot strawberry jelly
Mix the sugar and pectin NH together.
In a blender, blend the pre-cooked beetroot into a puree.
Heat the beetroot puree and strawberry puree together to 40 °C and add the sugar pectin mixture and the maltodextrin.
When the mixture boils, add the glucose and citric acid crystals and boil the jelly at 102.5 °C.
Add the vinegar and leave to cool down.
Pipe the jelly into the pre-molded chocolate shells, filling to 1/3.

Horseradish ganache
Heat the fresh cream with the maltodextrin, sorbitol crystals and glucose to 85 °C.
Pour over the Selection White Intense 31% chocolate and the cocoa butter.
Mix well with an immersion blender, then add the horseradish paste and mix again.
When the ganache cools to 35 °C, add the cold butter and mix again with an immersion blender.
Make sure the ganache has cooled to 28 °C before filling the chocolate shells.
Leave to crystallize in a fridge for 12 hours at 16 °C with a relative humidity level below 60%.
Close the molds with tempered Selection White Intense 31% chocolate, leave to set, and unmold.

TIP ⟶ *If you don't have maltodextrin for the jelly, you can simply replace it with sugar. The jelly will be a bit sweeter.*
For the ganache you can leave the maltodextrin out.

Peanut olive oil and rosemary

Combining the velvety richness of Costa Rica 38% milk chocolate, the crunchy delight of peanuts, and the aromatic essence of rosemary-infused ganache and olive oil, this recipe offers a harmonious blend of flavors that promises a tantalizing culinary experience.

COMPONENTS

For 100 bonbons of 12 g
Molding
Rosemary olive oil ganache
Almond and peanut praline

CHOCOLATE AND BEER PAIRING

Vedett Extra White's citrus and coriander notes combine beautifully with the creamy Costa Rica 38% milk chocolate ganache and are enhanced by salted peanuts, olive oil, and rosemary.

INGREDIENTS

Molding
4 g/bonbon

Selection Milk 35% chocolate	500 g

Rosemary olive oil ganache
4 g/bonbon

milk	155 g
freshly chopped rosemary	10 g
Costa Rica 38% milk chocolate	270 g
extra-virgin olive oil	65 g

Almond and peanut praliné
4 g/bonbon

sugar	125 g
almonds, roasted and peeled	190 g
peanuts, salted	80 g
Costa Rica 38% milk chocolate	95 g
Pure Prime Pressed Cocoa Butter	15 g

PREPARATION

Molding
Color the mold with tempered yellow cocoa butter and spray some gold powder over it with a gold pump; leave to crystallize.
Heat the Selection Milk 35% chocolate to 45 °C and temper to 29 °C on a marble slab.
Mold the colored polycarbonate bonbon molds with the tempered chocolate.
Leave to set for one hour at 16 °C with a relative humidity level below 60% before you fill the molds.
Mold: Chocolate World CW1578

Rosemary oil ganache
Heat the milk together with the chopped rosemary and infuse for 10 minutes.
Heat again to 85 °C and pour, straining out the rosemary, over the Costa Rica 38% milk chocolate. Mix with a spatula to obtain a ganache.
Cool the ganache to 32 °C. Add the olive oil gradually and mix with an immersion blender.
Use the ganache at 28 °C.
Fill the mold halfway with the rosemary olive oil ganache and leave to crystallize for 2 hours before adding the almond peanut praliné on top.

Almond and peanut praliné
Make a dry caramel with the sugar.
Pour the caramelized sugar over the roasted almonds and the salted peanuts and leave to cool.
When cooled, mix the above mixture in a robot cutter to achieve a thick, semi-liquid paste. This mixture will be around 40 °C.
Melt and add the Costa Rica 38% milk chocolate and cocoa butter and mix.
Pour this filling on a marble slab and temper it to 26 °C.
Pipe this tempered praliné filling into the mold on top of the rosemary olive oil ganache.
As this is a double bonbon mold, put both sides against each other immediately and put some clamps on the molds to position them correctly and keep them together.
Put the double molds in a fridge at 4 °C for 10 minutes and then transfer them to a chocolate fridge at 16 °C.
Leave them to crystallize for about two hours and then unmold the peanut bonbons.
Store them in a cool, dry place at approximately 16 °C and a relative humidity below 60%.

Smoked bell pepper and spicy almond ravioli

The smokey bell pepper flavor with chili flakes contrasts with the robust Cameroon 45% milk chocolate to stand out in this delicious chocolate ravioli.

COMPONENTS

For 100 ravioli of 15 g
Smoked bell pepper ganache
Chili almond paste
Enrobing

CHOCOLATE AND BEER PAIRING

Troubadour Imperial Stout's rich, roasted malt and chocolate notes complement the smoky bell pepper ganache made with Cameroon 45% milk chocolate wonderfully, and are enhanced by the spicy kick of chili almond paste.

INGREDIENTS

Smoked bell pepper ganache
5 g/ravioli

cream (35% fat)	160 g
invert sugar	25 g
sorbitol crystals	10 g
smoked bell pepper powder	7 g
Cameroon 45% milk chocolate	220 g
Selection Dark Intense 65% chocolate	35 g
butter	25 g

Chili almond paste
6 g/ravioli

almond paste 50% (marzipan)	700 g
chili powder	12 g
sea salt	2 g

Enrobing
4 g/ravioli

Selection Dark Intense 65% chocolate	as needed

PREPARATION

Smoked bell pepper ganache
Heat the cream, invert sugar, sorbitol crystals and smoked bell pepper powder until the mixture reaches 85 °C.
Pour over the Cameroon 45% milk chocolate and the Selection Dark Intense 65% chocolate.
Mix with a spatula to obtain a ganache.
When the ganache reaches 35 °C, add the cold butter and mix with an immersion blender to create a smooth emulsion.
Cover the ganache with cling film and leave to crystallize at room temperature.
When it reaches the perfect consistency to pipe, use the ganache immediately.

Chili almond paste
Gently combine the almond paste with the chili powder and the sea salt.
Roll out the chili almond paste to 2 cm thick.
Put this on top of a ravioli mold and push gently into the cavities.
Fill the cavities with a bit of the ganache.
Place a second layer of 2 mm chili almond paste on top and push gently together.
Remove the excess chili almond paste and do the process again to make more ravioli.

TIP ⟶ *You can also make them with round fluted dough cutters one by one, as in the picture.*

Enrobing
Heat the Selection Dark Intense 65% chocolate to 48 °C and temper it on a marble slab to 29.4 °C.
Enrobe the ravioli and leave to crystallize for a couple of minutes at room temperature.
Decorate with tempered red-colored white chocolate and use a frozen stamp to make the design on top (see p. 64).
Leave the ravioli to crystallize completely at 16 °C for about two hours and with a relative humidity below 60%.

Cassis and thyme

Experience the rich, aromatic flavors of Vietnam 73% dark chocolate ganache, delicately infused with thyme and beautifully paired with vibrant cassis jelly. This exquisite combination promises to elevate your bonbon experience to new heights.

COMPONENTS

For 150 bonbons of 12 g
Molding
Cassis jelly
Thyme chocolate ganache

CHOCOLATE AND BEER PAIRING

Rodenbach Grand Cru's fruity, sour profile cleanses beautifully the citrus and acidic notes of Vietnam 73% dark chocolate ganache, enhanced by thyme, and the tart, earthy sweetness of cassis jelly.

INGREDIENTS

Molding
3 g/bonbon

Selection Dark Intense 65% chocolate	270 g

Cassis jelly
4 g/bonbon

pectin NH	8 g
sugar	50 g
water	80 g
sugar	300 g
cassis puree	500 g

Thyme chocolate ganache
5 g/bonbon

fresh thyme	25 g
water	30 g
sugar	95 g
cream (35% fat)	390 g
glucose	115 g
sorbitol crystals	25 g
Vietnam 73% dark chocolate	365 g
butter	25 g

PREPARATION

Molding
Color the mold with tempered black cocoa butter and dust with some silver powder. Leave to crystallize.
Heat the Selection Dark Intense 65% chocolate to 47 °C and temper to 29.4 °C on a marble slab. Mold the polycarbonate bonbon molds with the chocolate.
Leave to set for one hour at 16 °C with a relative humidity level below 60% before you fill them.
Mold: Chocolate World CW12024

Cassis jelly
Combine the sugar (50 g) and the pectin. Heat the water, sugar (300 g) and cassis puree to 50 °C. Add the sugar-pectin mixture and boil at 103 °C.
Pour the cooked jelly onto a steel tray and mix with a spatula to cool down the jelly.
When the temperature is around 40 °C, transfer the jelly to a plastic bowl and cover with cling film. Let cool to room temperature.
Fill the chocolate mold with the jelly to 1/3.

TIP ⟶ *You can store leftover jelly in the freezer for another batch of cassis bonbons.*

Thyme chocolate ganache
Soak the thyme in the water and leave to infuse for 30 minutes. Put this mixture in a pan and add the sugar. Boil until it reaches a blond caramel color.
In the meantime, heat the cream until it reaches at least 80 °C.
Stop the caramelization process by adding the heated cream. Strain this warm mixture through a sieve and weigh the liquid. You should have 485 g in total.
If you don't have enough liquid, add some milk to obtain the 485 g.
Add the glucose and the sorbitol crystals and reheat to 85 °C.
Pour this over the Vietnam 73% dark chocolate.
To ensure good crystallization, make sure the ganache does not exceed 38 °C.
When the ganache reaches 35 °C, add cold butter and mix with an immersion blender.
When the ganache reaches 30 °C, pipe it on top of the cassis jelly.
Leave to crystalize for 12 hour in a cool dry place at 16 °C. Close with tempered Selection Dark Intense 65% chocolate and leave to crystalize. Demold the bonbons.

Crispy Vietnam Clove mandarin

Experience an unforgettable symphony of the clove's warmth, hazelnut's richness, citrus notes of the mandarin and the intensity of the Vietnam 73% dark chocolate.

BONBON BEER PAIRING

COMPONENTS

For 160 bonbons of 80 g
Clove hazelnut praliné
Framed clove praliné filling
Mandarin Vietnam ganache

CHOCOLATE AND BEER PAIRING

Westmalle Tripel's fruity and spicy taste pairs nicely with the Vietnam 73% dark chocolate ganache. The clove adds warmth, while the mandarin peel gives a fresh, zesty touch and ties everything together.

INGREDIENTS

Clove hazelnut praliné

sugar	260 g
water	60 g
hazelnuts, peeled	270 g
clove powder	3 g

Framed clove praliné filling 3 g/bonbon

Selection Milk 35% chocolate	150 g
Pure Prime Pressed Cocoa Butter	40 g
clove hazelnut praliné	500 g
Selection Dark Intense 65% chocolate	as needed

Mandarin Vietnam ganache 3 g/bonbon

cream (35% fat)	375 g
mandarin zest	12 g
sugar	120 g
sorbitol crystals	45 g
invert sugar	60 g
Vietnam 73% dark chocolate	450 g
butter	60 g
Mandarine Napoleon (optional)	15 g
Selection Dark Intense 65% chocolate	as needed

PREPARATION

Clove hazelnut praliné
Combine the sugar and water in a pan and heat to 118 °C.
Remove from the heat and add the hazelnuts.
Mix with a spatula until a sandy consistency is obtained.
Return to the heat and caramelize, stirring continuously with a spatula.
When caramelized, add the clove powder and pour onto a silicone sheet.
After cooling, grind the mixture in a robot cutter until a fine paste is formed; do not overheat.
Keep the clove hazelnut praliné in a dry place at room temperature for the next step.

Framed clove praliné filling
Heat the Selection Milk 35% chocolate and the cocoa butter to approximately 45 °C and mix in the clove praliné.
Temper the clove praliné filling to 24 °C on a marble slab.
Put a thin layer of tempered Selection Dark Intense 65% chocolate on a sheet of baking paper and put a frame of 37 x 27 cm and 6 mm high on top.
Pour the clove praliné filling into the frame and leave to crystallize for about 10 minutes in a cold fridge of 5 °C before adding the mandarin Vietnam ganache on top.

Mandarin Vietnam ganache
Use a microplane to get mandarin zest.
Heat the cream with the mandarin zest to 80 °C.
Dry caramelize the sugar and add the pre-heated cream, sorbitol crystals and invert sugar.
Reheat the whole mixture to 85 °C and pour over the Vietnam 73% dark chocolate.
Mix with a spatula until you have a nice emulsion.
When the ganache cools to 35 °C, add the cold butter and mix with an immersion blender.
Add the Mandarine Napoleon and mix again.
Put another 6 mm-high frame on top of the previous one and pour the ganache at 32 °C over the crystallized clove praliné.
Leave to crystallize for 12 hours at 16 °C and a relative humidity below 60%.
Cut squares with a guitar and enrobe with tempered Selection Dark Intense 65% chocolate (2 g/bonbon), then immediately put a transfer sheet on top.
Leave to crystallize for minimum two hours before removing the transfer sheet.
Store at 16 °C and an average humidity below 60%.

Chocolate rosemary lollipops

A perfect chocolate product, welcome at any festive occasion. A mix of sweet and salty, the earthy undertones of the rosemary harmonize with the blend of two Costa Rica chocolates.

COMPONENTS

For 20 lollipops of 15 g
Sugared rosemary
Dark chocolate discs
Milk chocolate drizzle

CHOCOLATE AND BEER PAIRING

De Ranke XX Bitter's hoppy and malty bitterness with citrus complements the smooth cooked milk and vanilla notes of Costa Rica 38% milk chocolate, while sweet rosemary adds a unique herbal touch to the chocolate lolly.

INGREDIENTS

Sugared rosemary
2 g/portion

fresh rosemary	25 g
water	25 g
sugar	75 g

Dark chocolate discs
3 g/portion

Costa Rica 64% dark chocolate	150 g

Milk chocolate drizzle
10 g/portion

Costa Rica 38% milk chocolate	300 g
sea salt	as needed
sugared rosemary	as needed

PREPARATION

Sugared rosemary
Wash the rosemary and chop into very small pieces with a sharp knife.
Combine the water with the sugar and bring to a boil.
When the sugar syrup reaches 117 °C, add the freshly chopped rosemary.
Continue heating, stirring continuously with a spatula.
When the mixture turns dry, keep stirring with a spatula for a minute.
Do not allow to caramelize.
Pour on a silicone sheet and leave to cool.
Store in a closed container.

Dark chocolate discs
Heat the Costa Rica 64% dark chocolate to approximately 48 °C and temper on a marble slab to 30 °C.
Pipe 20 chocolate dots of 2 cm on a plastic sheet with some space between each dot.
Immediately place a second plastic sheet on top and push the plastic down with a finger.
Push in the center of each chocolate dot to obtain chocolate discs with a diameter of 4 cm.
Leave to crystallize in a cool, dry place for about 30 minutes.
Unmold the chocolate discs from the plastic sheets.

Milk chocolate drizzle
Heat the Costa Rica 38% milk chocolate to approximately 45 °C and temper on a marble slab to 29 °C.
Draw circles of 8 cm on a sheet of baking paper with some space in between.
Drizzle some tempered milk chocolate in the 8 cm circles.
Sprinkle the chocolate with some sugared rosemary and a bit of salt.
Place a wooden skewer across the center of each circle and pipe some more tempered milk chocolate over it.
Immediately place a dark chocolate disc on top and leave the lollipop to crystallize for about 30 minutes before serving.

Kadayif pistachio bar

A wonderful bar full of texture. The rich pistachio taste in combination with crunchy baked Kadayif is heavenly. A pinch of salt completes the full palette of flavors that the Selection Milk 35% chocolate enhances beautifully.

COMPONENTS

For 5 bars of 100 g
Molding
Dubai-style filling

CHOCOLATE & BEER PAIRING

Brugse Zot Dubbel's rich caramel malt and subtle bitterness with dark fruit flavors complements the creamy sweetness of milk chocolate and the nutty, buttery notes of the Dubai pistachio chocolate bar.

INGREDIENTS

Molding
40 g/bar

Selection Milk 35% chocolate	500 g

Dubai-style filling
60 g/bar

kadayif	100 g
butter	25 g
Selection White Intense 31% chocolate	20 g
Pure Prime Pressed Cocoa Butter	10 g
Pistache praliné 52%	75 g
Pure pistachio paste	75 g
pure roasted sesame paste (tahin)	20 g
sea salt	1 g
roasted pistachio cubes	20 g

PREPARATION

Molding
Color bar molds with some colored and tempered cocoa butter and a little gold powder.
For coloring the molds, see basic techniques: "coloring of chocolate molds" p. 50.
Heat the Selection Milk 35% chocolate to 45 °C and temper it to 29 °C on a marble slab.
Mold the chocolate bar molds and leave to crystallize for about 30 minutes in a fridge at 16 °C with a relative humidity level below 60%.

Dubai-style filling
Cut the Kadayif into 1 cm pieces and bake in a pan with the butter until golden brown; set aside to cool.
Heat the Selection White Intense 31% chocolate and the cocoa butter to 43 °C.
Temper this composition at 28.5 °C.
Add the pistache praliné 52% and the pure pistachio paste and mix with a spatula.
Add all other ingredients and mix well.
Fill the chocolate bar molds and leave to crystallize for about 30 minutes.
Close the Dubai-style bars with tempered Selection Milk 35% chocolate.

Cheers & Chillers

Hot and cold chocolate cherry beer drink

Treat yourself to something unique. Crafted with single-origin Vietnam 73% chocolate, our unique hot and cold chocolate drink combines this fruity bitter chocolate with rich cherry beer and a luscious beer foam. Cheers!

COMPONENTS

For approximately 5 servings
Chocolate cherry beer drink
Cherry beer foam

CHOCOLATE & BEER PAIRING

Kriek Mystic Beer balances sweet and sharp sour flavors with ripe cherry notes and hints of almond. In a chocolate drink, it pairs perfectly with the complex fruity citrus notes of Vietnam 73% dark chocolate in a chocolate drink.

INGREDIENTS

Chocolate cherry beer drink 160 ml

Kriek Mystic	500 g
cream (35% fat)	100 g
Vietnam 73% dark chocolate	120 g
Vietnam 45% milk chocolate	80 g

Cherry beer foam (optional) 10 g

Kriek Mystic	125 g
albumin (egg white powder)	1 g

PREPARATION

Chocolate cherry beer drink
Bring the cherry beer to a brief boil and add the cream.
Pour this warm mixture on both chocolates and mix with an immersion blender until smooth.
Serve at 70 °C.

Cherry beer foam (optional)
In a stand mixer with a whisk, whip the cherry beer and the albumin powder until fluffy and stable.
Spoon some cherry beer foam onto the chocolate drink.

TIP ⟶ *The chocolate cherry beer drink can be served hot or cold. If serving cold, you can even add ice cubes.*

Cocoa beer frappé

The very idea of this intriguing and delicious drink leaves your mouth watering. Experience the perfect blend of cocoa, sweet milk, and beer married with the full flavor of Brussels Beer Project's zero New England IPA, Pico Bello (0.3% ABV) in our cocoa beer frappé. A refreshing, bold and creamy treat for all occasions.

COMPONENTS

For 3 frappés of 250 ml
Cocoa beer frappé

CHOCOLATE AND BEER PAIRING

The malty richness of Pico Bello beer, a hazy zero-ABV IPA with fruity aromas, a touch of bitterness, and a refreshing acidity, blends harmoniously with the bittersweet cocoa powder. The condensed milk adds a creamy sweetness, creating a refreshing frappé.

INGREDIENTS

Cocoa beer frappé
250 ml/serving

Premium Dutch Cocoa Powder	30 g
ice cubes	200 g
Brussels Beer Project Pico Bello	300 g
condensed sweet milk	120 g
full fat milk	100 g

PREPARATION

Cocoa beer frappé
In a milkshake blender, blend the cocoa powder, ice cubes, cold beer and condensed sweet milk for 1 minute starting at low speed to break the ice cubes. Finish blending at high speed.
Add the full-fat milk and blend for another 30 seconds at high speed.
Pour the frappé into a big glass.
Whisk some leftover beer with a whisk.
Take the foam with a spoon and transfer it on top of the cocoa beer frappé.
Serve and consume immediately.

Acknowledgements

I would like to express my deepest gratitude to Puratos for providing me with numerous challenges and opportunities that have shaped me into the professional I am today, and for their support in creating this book.

I would like to thank my wife, Valerie, for her patience and for giving me the freedom to express my passion for the work I do in chocolate and patisserie. I am also grateful for the countless hours she spent meticulously reading this book before its publication.

A big thanks to Lannoo Publishing — Johan Ghysels, Heidi Verschaeve and Inge Van Damme — for believing in this concept and giving me the chance to create this book and present it to all the passionate chefs out there.

The pictures in this book had a tremendous impact on the final product. Countless thanks must go to Karl Bruninx for the wonderful work he did in creating all these images.

I consulted Culinary Chef Sébastian Patte to help me create and put together the starters and main dishes. Thank you, Chef!

Thanks to beer specialist Werner Callebaut for providing me invaluable support and advice on the beer pairings for my recipes.

Thank you, Belcolade, for providing me with sustainable Belgian Chocolate of exceptional refinement and flavor.

A word of thanks to all Belgian beer brewers, who continuously strive to uphold the image of Belgian beer by consistently delivering the best quality brews.

A final word of thanks to all my current Technical Advisor colleagues, especially: Stéphane Leroux, Stef Aerts, Jeffrey De Weyer and Alessandro Nirchio.

www.lannoo.com
Register on our website and we will regularly send you a newsletter
with information about new books and interesting, exclusive offers.

Text: Michel Eyckerman
Photography: Karl Bruninx
Graphical design: Inge Van Damme

If you have observations or questions, please contact our editorial office:
redactielifestyle@lannoo.com

D/2025/45/398 - NUR 440
ISBN: 978 90 209 7861 2

Conversion Table

WEIGHTS FOR DRY INGREDIENTS

7 g	¼ oz
15 g	½ oz
20 g	¾ oz
25 g	1 oz
40 g	1½ oz
50 g	2 oz
60 g	2½ oz
75 g	3 oz
100 g	3½ oz
125 g	4 oz
150 g	5 oz
175 g	6 oz
200 g	7 oz
225 g	8 oz
250 g	9 oz
300 g	11 oz
350 g	12 oz
400 g	14 oz
450 g	1 lb
500 g	1 lb 2 oz
550 g	1¼ lb
600 g	1 lb 5 oz
650 g	1 lb 7 oz
700 g	1 lb 9 oz
750 g	1 lb 11 oz
800 g	1¾ lb
900 g	2 lb
1 kg	2¼ lb

LIQUID MEASURES

METRIC	IMPERIAL	US
25 ml	1 fl oz	
50 ml	2 fl oz	¼ cup
75 ml	3 fl oz	
100 ml	3½ fl oz	
120 ml	4 fl oz	½ cup
150 ml	5 fl oz	
175 ml	6 fl oz	¾ cup
200 ml	7 fl oz	
250 ml	8 fl oz	1 cup
300 ml	10 fl oz/½ pint	1¼ cups
400 ml	14 fl oz	
450 ml	15 fl oz	2 cups/1 pint
600 ml	1 pint	2½ cups
750 ml	1¼ pints	
900 ml	1½ pints	
1 litre	1¾ pints	1 quart

OVEN TEMPERATURES

°C	°F
110	225
120	250
140	275
150	300
160	325
180	350
190	375
200	400
220	425
230	450
240	475